Dan

The Battle of Alberta

Now,
That your old
enough you have the
right to know more
about this amazing game
and on going battle!
Happy 40th B-day buddy

Love Celeste &
Joel

The Battle of Alberta
A Century of Hockey's Greatest Rivalry

Steven Sandor

Victoria · Calgary · Vancouver

Heritage House Publishing Company Ltd.
#108 – 17665 66A Avenue
Surrey, BC V3S 2A7
www.heritagehouse.ca

1 2 3 4 5 / 08 07 06 05

Library and Archives Canada Cataloguing in Publication

Sandor, Steven, 1971-
   The battle of Alberta : a century of hockey's greatest
rivalry / Steven Sandor.
Includes index.

ISBN 1-894974-01-8

   1. Hockey--Alberta--History. I. Title.
GV848.4.C3S25 2005   796.96'2'097123   C2005-904718-6

Edited by Linda Berry and Corina Skavberg
Book design by One Below
Cover design by One Below
Front cover photo: (left) Courtesy of Calgary Stampede Historical Committee
                   (right) Glenbow Archives NC-6-7064
                   (background) Glenbow Archives NA-3965-49
Back cover photo: (left) Courtesy of the Calgary Flames Hockey Club
                   (right) The Edmonton Journal

Printed in Canada on 100% post-consumer recycled paper.

Heritage House acknowledges the financial support for its publishing program from the Government of Canada through the Book Publishing Industry Development Program (BPIDP), Canada Council for the Arts, and the British Columbia Arts Council.

Canada Council **Conseil des Arts**
for the Arts **du Canada**

BRITISH COLUMBIA
ARTS COUNCIL
Supported by the Province of British Columbia

Acknowledgements

This book would not be possible if not for the enthusiastic support of many who have helped make the Battle of Alberta the most revered sports rivalry in Western Canada. I would like to thank the following players, managers and fans for agreeing to be interviewed for this book, or for giving me their time after pre-game skates, practices and in post-game scrums.

Doug Barkley
Perry Berezan
Dave Brown
Kelly Buchberger
Pat Conacher
Shean Donovan
Don Edwards
Cliff Fletcher
Grant Fuhr
Mike Grier
Glenn Hall
Charlie Huddy
Dave Hunter
Tim Hunter
Jarome Iginla
Lou Jankowski
Mike Krushelnyski
Lyle "Sparky" Kulchisky
Patrick LaForge
Ron "Squeak" Leopold

Ken Linseman
Kevin Lowe
Jamie Macoun
Craig MacTavish
Kevin McClelland
Lanny McDonald
Derek Morris
Joe Mullen
Kirk Muller
Craig Muni
Bob Murdoch
Joel Otto
Jim Peplinski
Frank Roggeveen
Craig Simpson
Ron Stern
Darryl Sutter
Stéphane Yelle
Zarley Zalapski

As well, this book would not have been possible without the assistance of Bill Tuele of the Edmonton Oilers and Peter Hanlon of the Calgary Flames. They both have offered outstanding assistance over the years to a young hockey writer looking to cover the greatest game in the world.

I would also like to thank Professor Michael P.J. Kennedy at the University of Saskatchewan, for convincing me that writing this book was the right thing to do.

Table of Contents

Foreword

It is the morning of Game 3 of the Calgary Flames' first-round playoff series against the Vancouver Canucks. The mood of the city is buoyant; the Olympic flame atop the Calgary Tower has been relit. Flames fans zoom down 17th Avenue S—the "Red Mile" to anyone who knows the city—honking their car horns and waving red, white and gold flags out their windows. The 2004 playoffs are the first time the Flames have made it to the post-season since they were swept in the first round in 1996 by the Chicago Blackhawks.

At the Pengrowth Saddledome, a long red-and-burnt-orange banner flies right outside the doors of the Flames' dressing room, in full view of the players as they walk from the ice. On it are hundreds of signatures wishing the team luck. Even though the Edmonton Oilers are not the Flames' playoff opponent—in fact, the two teams haven't met in a playoff series since 1991—the banner is filled with notes claiming the "Oilers suck."

But somewhere near the Flaming C on the good-luck banner, a foul act of sabotage has occurred. In thick black marker, an anonymous Oilers fan has left a message for the Flames...

"My two favourite teams are the Oilers and whoever plays the Flames! Go Oil!" it reads.

Even though the Flames are about to play their first playoff home game in eight years—against the Vancouver Canucks, no less—there is no escaping their greatest rival, those Edmonton Oilers.

There is probably no place in the world that embraces hockey like Canada. Originally played on frozen rivers, ponds, lakes and sloughs across the country, the game is really a product of our long winters. Canadians needed something to help them endure the tedium—hockey was our tonic.

There is no place in Canada that embraces the game of hockey quite like Alberta. Despite not having anything close to the population of Ontario or Quebec, Alberta supports two National Hockey League clubs, a fully stocked Alberta Junior Hockey League and four separate Western Hockey League junior franchises in Calgary, Red Deer, Lethbridge and Medicine Hat.

But our greatest hockey love is the modern Battle of Alberta; the Calgary Flames and Edmonton Oilers have forged one of the most heated rivalries in all of professional sport. Modern NHL fans may point to the ongoing hostilities between the Colorado Avalanche and Detroit Red Wings or the Battle of Ontario between the Toronto Maple Leafs and Ottawa Senators as the greatest rivalries in the game. With no offence meant towards those fine teams, these rivalries don't hold a candle to the Oilers and Flames when they squared off during their glory years.

We still observe the Battle of Alberta; the Oilers and Flames, barring NHL labour strife, are still solid divisional rivals. They are the most obvious reflection of the differences between Alberta's two major cities. Calgary has always been Alberta's big-playing metropolitan centre; it is Alberta's financial nerve centre and the home to the province's biggest moneymaker, the oil industry. Edmonton is the more liberal government and university town. It is the capital and home to Canada's second-largest post-secondary institution, the University of Alberta. Where Calgary is about big bucks and the Stampede, Edmonton is famous for cultural festivals and being the Gateway to the North.

Since the Flames did not come to Calgary until 1980, it's foolish to believe that the Battle of Alberta began with their rivalry with the Oilers. In fact, Calgary and Edmonton hockey teams have battled each other for more than a century. Long before Alberta was declared a province by Sir Wilfrid Laurier's Liberals in 1905, hot-blooded hockey matches between amateur Edmonton and Calgary clubs littered the sports pages of those cities' papers. After the conclusion of the Second World War, the two Alberta cities ushered in a new golden age for hockey in the province; the Calgary Stampeders and Edmonton Flyers both won Allan Cups (in '46 and '48, respectively), the trophy of the national senior amateur championship. Teams from Edmonton and Calgary vied for the Stanley Cup even before the National Hockey League came to Alberta.

Throughout the '50s and early '60s, Edmonton and Calgary were just one step away from the NHL. Each city played host to a top-tier minor pro team—Edmonton was affiliated with the Detroit Red Wings, while Calgary was linked with the Chicago Black Hawks. Some truly outstanding players, from Flyers stars Glenn Hall, Norm Ullman and John Bucyk to Stamps legends Lou Jankowski, Ron "Squeak" Leopold and Doug Barkley, battled until pro hockey left the prairies about the same time as Beatlemania struck North America.

Yes, the Oilers and Flames defined the modern Battle of Alberta. But, in truth, the Battle has been a part of Alberta sporting life since the 19th century. This book is a salute to any player who has pulled on a Calgary or Edmonton hockey sweater and played in an Alberta classic. From Glenn Hall to Glenn Anderson, Lou Jankowski to Jim Peplinski, Duke Keats to the Great One, Alberta hockey fans can only say thank you for all the great memories.

Steven Sandor
Edmonton, May 2005

The Rivalry Begins

There are still some who believe that Canada's most emotionally charged hockey rivalry began in 1980, when Nelson Skalbania and a group of investors moved the Atlanta Flames to Calgary—giving the Edmonton Oilers a geographic rival. The modern Battle of Alberta between the Flames and the Oilers has been only the latest chapter in a longstanding battle on the ice between the province's two key cities. The story began in the late 19th century, when the region that would become Alberta was still part of the Northwest Territories, more than a decade away from being officially recognized as a province. Hockey had already captured the imagination of Canadians east of Winnipeg. Within months of the first recorded game in Edmonton in 1894, hockey had bumped curling as the main feature sport in the *Edmonton Bulletin*'s pages. Calgarians can point to the fact that the first recorded hockey game took place in their city in 1893, a year before Edmonton could make that claim.

And maybe, just maybe, one of the fur-clad spectators watching the young men playing hockey on the frozen

North Saskatchewan River whispered the words "Battle of Alberta" to describe the action on the ice, but it was not in reference to a game that saw one of the new Edmonton-based teams take on visitors from Calgary. In 1895, the Edmonton Thistles' greatest rival was a team of Northwest Mounted Police officers from the Fort Saskatchewan base. While Edmontonians were aware that there were some strong hockey clubs in Calgary, the members of the Northwest Mounted Police filled the pages of the *Edmonton Bulletin* with boasts that they were the best hockey team in the Dominion of Canada west of Winnipeg, and should challenge for a new national amateur hockey trophy, the Dominion Challenge Cup, that had just been donated by Lord Stanley of Preston. That Cup would later become better known by its affectionate nickname—the Stanley Cup.

A small notice in the November 29, 1894 edition of the *Edmonton Bulletin* signalled hockey's arrival in Edmonton. "A hockey club is being started both here and in south Edmonton,"[1] read the ad. "On account of the enclosed rink being too small and not built so a game can be played there, a rink is being made on the river the correct size, when no doubt some good sport will take place."

The first to hold organized practices were the Thistles, a team made up mainly of British-born aristocrats who wanted something a little more fast-paced than curling. At a time when "hockey boots" could be purchased at W.T. Henry & Co. for the princely sum of $2.50, the Thistles held their first meeting and named Inspector Snyder the captain of the team, with an eye to getting a competitive unit on the ice as quickly as possible. The South Edmonton Stars, the second team alluded to in the ad, were not ready to play as quickly as the Thistles, nor were they at the same level of skill as other teams. On Christmas Day, 1894, after a 150 ft by 75 ft rink—50 feet shorter than the current NHL regulation size—had been cleared near the ferry dock at the Fort Saskatchewan River, the first hockey game in history between two Edmonton teams took place, with the Mounties claiming a narrow 3–2 win over the Thistles.

The game was very different from the hockey we know today. The modern game is contested with five skaters and one goalie per side. Back then, each team played with six skaters and a goalie. Most teams employed three of the skaters as forwards, while the other three players could be assigned to "point" or "cover point" positions. In the modern game, players jump over the boards to change either on the fly or during a stoppage in play. In 1894, there were no substitutions in the game. The NWMP and the Thistles each came to the rink with seven players. Each player would be expected to be on the ice for both halves of the game. A hockey game divided into three periods was an innovation that would not arrive for another 15 years. The players didn't whip a puck around the ice either. They played with a ball, so bounces were unpredictable at best.

The game was such a success that the Fort and the Thistles agreed to play an entire series of games through the winter of 1894–95. On New Year's Day, the Fort prevailed once again with a 2–1 win. But the Thistles knuckled down and won the next two games, each by 3–2 scores. After four games, the NWMP and the Thistles had each won twice, and had each scored the same number of goals over the series. A fifth game was held, and after a lengthy overtime that lasted until the game was called on account of darkness, the sides settled for a 2–2 draw.

A team called the Edmonton Citizens then challenged the Mounties and won by a 5–1 score. The game was not nearly as ballyhooed as the matches between the Thistles and the NWMP, so there was no doubt embarrassment in both the Thistles' and Mounties' camps that an unheralded team with little history could embarrass one of the better-known Edmonton teams.

With both the Thistles and the NWMP gaining in popularity throughout Edmonton, a team from Calgary agreed to make the trek north to take on both of these new clubs. It would mark the first time that an officially recorded game would take place between Calgary and Edmonton teams. At the time of the games, Calgary and Edmonton were two rival towns in Alberta, which was a sparsely populated section of the Northwest Territories. To say that Calgary and Edmonton were major centres at the time would be an exaggeration. According to an 1896 census by J.B. Spurr, Edmonton's population stood at 1,267 souls, spiraling upward from an estimated 500 as recorded in the 1891 federal census. Meanwhile, the 1891 census pegged Calgary and the surrounding area at just around 4,000 citizens.

The hockey scenes were radically different in the two cities. Games in Edmonton were organized affairs. Large crowds clamoured to see the Thistles and NWMP, clubs that were made up of either officers or gentlemen. The Thistles were comprised of British members of the Edmonton elite; it was like a country club on ice. Meanwhile, a small three-team league had established itself in Calgary, made up of the Fire Brigade, the Calgary Club (often referred to as the

"Ranchers") and a team called the Maple Leafs, referred to as the "Israelites" by one *Edmonton Bulletin* writer.

According to early game reports in the *Calgary Herald*, these league games were often plagued by poor turnouts of "cranks" (fans) and did not stir as much excitement as the local teams did in Edmonton. But what Calgary lacked in fan fervour, it more than made up when it came to on-ice participation. While hockey in Edmonton was limited to the blue-blooded clubs, amateur clubs filled Calgary's ice. Besides the Ranchers, Israelites and Fire Brigade ice teams, there were many newspaper reports of teams from various religious organizations and community groups. Even the *Herald* had its own team. Local printers had a team called the Picas, and a report from the *Herald* showed the state of hockey in the city at the time: "But at times, some of the printers, who had never handled a hockey stick before, played with little regards to the rules of the game."[2] In Calgary, hockey was not restricted to those with privilege; anyone who wanted to grab a stick and lace up a pair of skates could contribute to the growth of the game in the town, and they could also make headlines!

In the first week of March, 1895, a Calgary all-star team made up of the best players from that city (all but one of the skaters came from the Fire Brigade squad) faced both the Thistles and Mounties, and the Edmontonians were humbled. Neither the Thistles nor the NWMP could get a shot past a Calgary goaltender by the name of Wilson. Calgary took the Thistles by a 1–0 margin and then beat the Mounties 2–0. Edmontonians weren't the only ones shocked by the results; Calgarians also considered it an upset. At that time, gentlemanly wagers between teams were commonplace, but before the series in Edmonton, the Calgary All-Stars were not in a betting mood, a sign that they didn't fancy their own chances before the games began.

"The north clubs expected to win, but take their defeat willingly," read a game report in the *Calgary Herald*. "Not much money changed hands, as the Calgary sports either lacked confidence in their clubs or the necessary lucre."[3]

An early spring thaw marred the games. When Calgary arrived, the river ice was already soft. The games were affected by mushy ice which caused the ball to bounce strangely—modern NHLers who complain about ice conditions in rinks in the southern United States should take a look at the history of the game to see that bad ice has always plagued the sport! Those Calgary visits marked the end of the season; the spring thaw had determined that no games of consequence would occur until the next winter.

The Fort Saskatchewan/Thistles rivalry picked up again in earnest on Christmas Day, 1895—the designated opening day of hockey season. The Thistles won the opener over the NWMP by a 4–2 count, setting up the most heated rematch ever held between the two teams. On New Year's Day, 1896, the Thistles and Mounties played in their fiercest game to date. The Mounties won 3–2, but the January 2nd edition of the *Edmonton Bulletin* had nothing but disdain for a game that editor Frank Oliver saw as nothing more than police brutality. Captain Fulton of the Thistles pulled his team off the ice to protest the put-the-whistle-in-the-pocket attitude of referee Reverend D'Easum.

"It is too bad if a game like hockey, which is becoming very popular, and in this northern country where the sport can be played longer than in other parts, is to be spoiled by rough playing. It is in the interest of the game that in the future a firm referee who will make both side (sic) adhere strictly to the rules be appointed. The Thistles cannot speak too highly of the gentlemanly way in which the police treated them off the ice, but do complain that they did not play hockey on it."[4]

While the rivalry was heated, neither team lost its sense of honour. After an 1896 game that the Fort won by a 1–0 score, the two teams gathered for a rifle-shooting match, which the Thistles won.

As the hockey season of 1895–96 drew to a close, both the NWMP and the Thistles were eager to have rematches against opposition from Calgary. A tournament was organized that would feature an All-Star team from Calgary (loaded with players from their famous Fire Brigade squad) along with the South Edmonton Stars, the Edmonton Shamrocks and the new Victoria Club from Fort Saskatchewan. The tournament, which began on February 14th, 1896, should have been called the St. Valentine's Day Massacre. What was meant to be a platform for revenge for both the NWMP and the Thistles quickly turned to humiliation at the hands of the Calgarians. The NWMP's claims that they had the best team west of Winnipeg were shattered forever as they were hammered 9–1 by Calgary, hot on the heels of Calgary's 8–0 drubbing of the Thistles. The Calgarians would fire 12 goals into the Shamrocks net as well, easily claiming the gold pins given to the tournament champions. "The Thistles played hard," stated the game report in the *Edmonton Bulletin*. "But the Calgary men played by far the most scientific game and kept the puck nearly all the time at the Thistles goal."[5]

Despite the blowout score, there was no sign that things would ever get uncivilized between the Thistles and Calgary. "Although the game was hard-fought throughout, there was nothing but fair play on the part of either team," claimed the *Bulletin*'s game report.

While fans hotly followed the games in Edmonton, where reports made the front pages of the paper and crowds jammed the rink to see their hometown heroes—Calgarians were not nearly as excited. The day after the massacre in Edmonton, there was indeed a hockey story on the front page of the *Calgary Herald*. It was a report on the Stanley Cup challenge game which saw the Winnipeg Victorias upset the defending champion Montreal Victorias. The Alberta games did get some mention, but they were not followed with nearly the same interest as they were in the north.

The early games established hockey on the western border of the Canadian prairies, and also served as an important diversion for the people of the region. As the first Edmonton/Calgary games were played, the spectre of war hung over the small Northwest Territories' population.

At the end of 1895, Venezuela disputed its border with British Guiana. With the British offering little in terms of a diplomatic solution, the Venezuelans asked the United States to intervene on their behalf. President Grover Cleveland agreed to enter the fray; the Americans justified their involvement by citing the Monroe Doctrine, their standing foreign policy which stated they could intervene in any conflict within the United States' sphere of influence.

As the British forces were occupied with the growing conflict in South Africa, which would escalate into the Boer War by 1899, the American war hawks saw that the time was ripe to strike. Naturally, the first target would have been Canada: it was still loyal to the Crown and had vast tracts of sparsely populated land ripe for invasion. Despite their small population, Canadians were ready to fight the Americans, if need be. Frank Oliver wrote that Americans should be warned that Canada would not change loyalties if the growing Venezuela crisis escalated to war between Britain and the United States. "One thing which has been shown as a result of the Venezuela war scare is that there is no sentiment in Canada in favor of political union with the United States."[6]

Those pro-Crown sympathies were reflected in Calgary. "Canada will be foremost in the field, fighting for the empire of which she forms a part," promised the *Calgary Herald.* "There will be no division in her ranks. Her settlers one and all will be found side by side with the soldiers of the Queen, and with the memories of Queenstown Heights and Lundy's Lane before them, will testify by their blood if necessary, their unswerving loyalty to the old country and the world-wide empire of which they are so proud."[7]

As the winter of 1896 wore on, Germany joined the United States in publicly chastising Britain for its foreign policy. Even as the hockey teams played on, the players knew they could be called to serve in war.

"The British Empire has grown so great in its dependencies—and Canada more than any other dependency—must be prepared to play their several parts in the game," stated the *Edmonton Bulletin.* "Otherwise the Empire has become too unwieldy to stand successfully a combined attack such as was in prospect only a week ago; and may yet become a fact."[8]

War unites people of different political stripes like nothing else. Using the Venezuela Crisis and the possibility of an invasion of Canada as proof that Edmonton and Calgary were united on many issues is a bit of a reach. But, truly, Calgary and Edmonton were united on most of the major issues of the time. Both cities supported the opening of the West to European settlers looking for land. Calgary and Edmonton both pushed to have Alberta gain its provincial status. If there was any issue that divided the cities, it was the railroad. The Canadian Pacific Railway may have been the iron thread that held the new country together, but farmers across the Northwest Territories wanted an alternative to the CPR. Edmonton wanted a railway of its own (the CPR's main line went through Calgary). Calgarians agreed that new railways would be needed, but they believed that any new links should be made southbound to the American border, where farmers could realize more profits by selling their goods south of the border. While both cities knew that having Alberta recognized as a province would help the quest for more rail connections, they disagreed over which city should be the hub of any new Alberta railway—and if the line should go east/west or north/south.

Oliver, as a former Northwest Territories legislator and future MP, was a loud voice in favour of Edmonton-friendly rail routes. But the rival *Herald* took joy in poking fun at his pro-Edmonton proposals and at the fact that the newspaperman was leading a political double life. After Oliver criticized one of the *Herald*'s editorials in support of the north/south route, the Calgarians returned fire.

"The gentleman who presides over the destinies of the *Edmonton Bulletin* does not appear to be able to read correctly articles which appear in other newspapers. This is not to be unexpected seeing that his opportunities for keeping up with the times are necessarily limited."9

By 1897, the Edmonton Shamrocks had surpassed the NWMP as the Thistles' main local rival. In fact, the Shamrocks quickly established themselves as the best club in the city and earned an invitation in the winter of 1898 to travel to Calgary to take part in a tournament being held in conjunction with that city's famous annual curling bonspiel. That's when the Calgary/Edmonton rivalry turned bloody, setting the stage for the next 100 years and more.

The Calgary Fire Brigade had regularly humiliated Edmonton opposition ever since the two cities started sending teams to play against each other. The Shamrocks gave notice that the Fire Brigade might be in for a change in fortunes when they won the first game of the Calgary tournament by an impressive 7–1 count over the Town Boys (another Calgary team). The Shamrocks captured the championship the next day with a 6–5 squeaker over the Fire Brigade. Calgary's big guns had finally been silenced, but not without a heavy cost. Calgary's Everett Marshall had to have an eye removed after a Shamrock's stick smashed into his face. While the *Edmonton Bulletin* claimed it was an accident, the paper alluded to the fact that it set off a chain of ugly incidents throughout the game. "Several other players, including some of the Shamrocks were also, though, less seriously, injured."10 To be fair, it needs to be mentioned that Marshall had a history of eye injuries. Three years before, in a game against another Calgary club, Marshall was badly injured after taking a puck in the eye.11

Despite the bloody nature of the game, the Calgary Fire

Brigade accepted an invitation to contest the "Northern Alberta Championship" against the Thistles and Shamrocks in Edmonton a year later. The Calgarians arrived in Edmonton on February 13, 1899, thinking that the violence of the year before had been an isolated incident.

They were wrong.

The Shamrocks pummeled the Calgarians by a 13–4 count in the opening game, but once again it was violence that commanded the attention of the newspaper. "Within a minute after play commenced, Hunter, of the Calgary team, was knocked out by a blow over the left eye, supposed to be from a hockey stick."[12] To add insult to injury, Calgary was hammered the next night 15–2 by the Thistles. Unfortunately, unseasonably warm weather forced the postponement of the championship game between the two Edmonton sides. Within two winters, the Calgary Fire Brigade, once considered the best team in all of the Alberta territory, had been surpassed by both of Edmonton's big clubs.

The end of the century concluded with hockey still a friendly affair between the two cities. But the political and sporting rivalry between the two would come to a head in the coming years. As Alberta prepared for its official provincial status, the matters on ice would get a lot nastier between the two towns. The loss of an eye in a hockey game would only be the first incident in a long-standing hockey rivalry filled with blood, sweat and tears.

Capital Battles to the Great Default

As Alberta moved towards its 1905 inauguration as an official province, hostilities between Edmonton and Calgary increased. Calgary was larger and a hub on the Canadian Pacific Railway, whereas Edmonton had only a spur line that terminated in what was then known as Strathcona (now the Whyte Avenue district). According to a 1901 federal census of the Alberta territory, Edmonton East had a population of 1,157 and Edmonton West had 1,491 residents. These numbers included rural residents from the surrounding area. Calgary was almost twice as large as Edmonton. The same census showed that Calgary's six districts (two in the city centre, and the north, west, east and south districts) showed a total population of 4,871. Naturally, the city fathers in Alberta's budding city in the south believed they were the natural hosts of the new capital.

But Ottawa had other plans. Edmonton was well-represented by longtime Liberal Frank Oliver. The founder of the *Edmonton Bulletin,* Oliver was a captain in the Liberal

Party; he was elected to the House of Commons in 1896 and was named the Minister of the Interior in 1905. Oliver was also put in charge of Indian Affairs that same year. As the most influential MP in what was to be the new province, he regularly had the ear of Prime Minister Sir Wilfrid Laurier. Oliver rallied his city to push Ottawa for the right to be the provincial capital. Soon, federal money poured into Edmonton, much to the disdain of Calgarians.

"That is a laudable purpose of the Edmonton Board of Trade to boom Edmonton and let the world know it has been granted an appropriation of $14,000 by the government for a new jail," railed Calgary *Eye Opener* editor and Oliver opponent Bob Edwards in January of 1905, months before the feds were to make their final decision on the placement of the capital. "They are bent on having the capitol up there and are starting in early to whoop things up and build up their burg."[13]

As Edmonton's campaign for the capital increased, Edwards' disdain reflected the mood of his Calgary readers.

"Edmonton now estimates it has a population of 4,000," he wrote with his famous biting satire. "Estimates are easy to make. Calgary, with her bona fide population of 17,000, is seriously thinking of estimating her population at 25,000 just to prove its imagination is not inferior to Edmonton's.

"Edmonton's bid for the capital has had a disastrous effect. Okotoks, Claresholm, Olds, Carstairs, Cochrane and Ponoka have crept out gingerly from the underbrush and begun squeaking about their claims."[14]

Edwards and other Edmonton opponents were disheartened when Oliver and fellow Liberal Peter Talbot were put in charge of setting up the province's new electoral boundaries. The two decided—despite Calgary's large population—that northern Alberta would get 13 seats in the new legislature, which would be temporarily convened in Edmonton's Thistle Rink (usually a home for hockey). Calgary and the south would only get 12 seats. The Liberals, led by Alexander C. Rutherford, won 23 of those 25 seats in the election; in 1906, the new government defeated a motion from Calgary that the capital be located there, paving the way to affirm Edmonton as the permanent home of Alberta's seat of government.

The controversy over the capital soured relations between the two cities, and it can be argued that the politicking that gave Edmonton the seat of government is the seed for the malcontent that still exists between it and Calgary to this day. That bitterness spilled over into all things to do with both cities' favourite pastime—hockey. When the Alberta Amateur Hockey Association was formed in 1907, representatives from Calgary held out on joining the new governing body. Calgarians claimed that travel costs between itself and Edmonton were too prohibitive to have their teams going north and south across the province on a regular basis. But according to Alberta hockey historian Gary W. Zeman, Calgary's reluctance to join the AAHA may have been spurred by the fear of being further embarrassed by the new capital. "It is possible there was more to it than that. Edmonton was a 'powerhouse' and perhaps Calgary did not want to play in the same league."[15]

The Calgary holdout was only temporary; by 1910, the city was an active member of the AAHA. Then in 1913 Calgary and Edmonton got into a dispute that hammered home just how cold relations between the two cities had become on the hockey front.

The pre-First World War era was an especially scandalous time for the game. In 1908, the Edmonton Hockey Club, which played out of the Thistle Rink, became the first Alberta team to win the right to challenge for the Stanley Cup. At this time, the Stanley Cup was still emblematic of amateur hockey supremacy. But Edmonton scandalized the game by signing Tom Phillips, a two-time Cup winner with the Montreal AAA and the Rat Portage Thistles; Didier "Cannonball" Pitre, the man considered to have the hardest slapshot in the history of the game at the time; and Lester Patrick, who defected from the current Cup-holding Montreal Wanderers to lead the challenge against his former club. Basically, Edmonton manager Fred Whitcroft brought in an entirely new team of ringers to wage the battle for the Cup against the Wanderers. No one doubted that Whitcroft was paying the players under the table, and had in fact hired a pro team to take the place of his amateurs for the Cup final. Whitcroft's plan backfired, and the Wanderers defeated Edmonton to retain the Cup. Edmonton would also lose another Cup challenge, to the Ottawa Senators, in 1910.

The scandal illustrated the need for hockey officials to be more diligent in their efforts to weed pro players out of the amateur ranks. By 1909, with the formation of the National Hockey Association paving the way for entrenched pro hockey in Canada, the Stanley Cup had become a professional prize. The Allan Cup, a new trophy donated by Sir Montague Allan, became the new national amateur prize, governed by the Canadian Amateur Hockey Association. At that time, the Allan Cup was not far behind Lord Stanley's mug when it came to prestige. Because any community could create an amateur club that could make a run for the Allan Cup, there was a feeling that the Allan Cup was a truer national trophy than the Stanley Cup.

Deacon White, who founded the Edmonton Eskimos out of the ashes of the old Edmonton Hockey Club, badly wanted his club to be the first Alberta-based team to hoist the Allan Cup. To reach this goal, his club needed to win the Alberta amateur championship first. Standing in the Eskimos' way were the Calgary Shermans, so named for the fact that they played out of their city's Sherman Rink. As well, the Taber Cooks, named for the famous Cook family who ran the team, also posed a threat for the 1913 provincial title. The draw for the Alberta championship was simple: Edmonton would face Taber in a neutral-site venue (Calgary), and the winner would play the Shermans for the right to try and issue an Allan Cup challenge to the current holders, the Winnipeg Victorias.

Even though more than 2,000 fans jammed the Sherman Rink, many of them partisan fans from Edmonton who made the journey south to cheer on their team, the Eskimos could not capitalize on their unofficial home ice advantage. Thanks to some outstanding play from the Cook brothers, Taber won the game 6–4 and the Eskimos were eliminated from the Alberta playoff picture. Or were they? At the time, the Alberta amateur hockey scene was a dirty and under-handed business. Teams regularly paid pros to play as amateurs, and hoped that the AAHA would either not notice or look the other way.

The Shermans would not be so lucky. Taber urged the

AAHA to investigate Shermans star Tommy Piette, who they claimed was really pro Tommy Thompson playing under an assumed name. They were correct, but in his admission to the authorities, Thompson said that Taber had known all along that he was at one time a for-hire player, but had waited until the timing was right to press charges. Still, the AAHA had no choice but to bar Piette/Thompson from further play.

After the disqualification, the two teams met on February 28 for the first game in what was supposed to be a best-of-three series for the provincial championship. Thanks to the stellar play of Shermans netminder Charlie McCarthy, the Shermans eked out a 3-2 win. But as the series was played, the Eskimos urged the Alberta Amateur Hockey Association into an investigation of Taber's Lloyd Cook, another of the famous brothers. The AAHA found that Cook had also played pro hockey in British Columbia. Frustrated by the shenanigans, the AAHA decided to cancel the rest of the playoff series and disqualify Taber from the play-offs—and ordered the Shermans, without Piette, to face the Eskimos in a new Alberta final.

Lloyd Turner, the manager of the Shermans, was incensed by the decision. He claimed that White had bamboozled the AAHA to allow his team, which had already lost, back into the competition. "The players and management cannot see in any way why they should play the Eskimos and will not play them this season," read the story in the *Calgary Herald* the next day.[16] Turner also faced losing major gate money as the Shermans' home game against Taber was already sold out. He promised that his team would rather default to the Eskimos than be subjected to the AAHA's justice. Turner made good on his promise, and the AAHA declared the Eskimos, who had not won a single playoff game, the provincial champions and backed Edmonton's Allan Cup challenge.

Meanwhile, the Cooks, who were refused the right to play even exhibition games against amateur teams, threatened to question the status of the Eskimos in the lineup. A.B. Cook promised that he would urge the AAHA to investigate the "amateurs" at White's disposal. "Regarding the charges laid against them by the Edmonton team, A.B. said very little but stated that he had just as much on the Edmonton players as they had on his team, and that he intended to go after them."[17]

The back-and-forth between the teams only proves just how dirty amateur hockey in Alberta had become at that point. The truth is that pretty well every amateur team at that time was using illegal players—men who were either being paid under the table or had played pro hockey elsewhere before agreeing to join one of the elite Alberta clubs. The crime wasn't to cheat, but to get caught.

For days after the default, Turner and White continued to attack each other in person and through the press. The *Edmonton Bulletin* got the chance to eavesdrop on an over-the-phone screaming match between Turner and White, and blasted the Calgarians for not playing the final. "Turner continued this report and gave several very halting excuses for his baby action," snarled the *Bulletin* report.[18] It claimed White barked that Turner was "yellow" for not sending his team north. The *Calgary Herald* reported that White thought the Shermans were scared to face the Eskimos because of how well the Edmonton club fared against its cross-city rivals, the Dominions. "The Deacon deliberately insinuated that as the Eskimos had twice beaten the Dominions, while Dominions in turn had trounced the Shermans, that perhaps the Shermans were a wee bit frightened to venture into a series with Mr. White's Allan Cup challengers."[19]

Soon after the Eskimos were declared Alberta champions, the Shermans asked that the AAHA reconsider and reschedule the games. After some sober second thought, Turner and his associates had decided it might be better for the Shermans to play the games, after all. "The latest story from Calgary would indicate that Shermans are already beginning to regret their somewhat hasty action of defaulting to the Eskimos," jeered an *Edmonton Bulletin* sports report.[20] "The team has not yet disbanded and the players claim that they received no official notification from the AAHA that they were to meet the Eskimos. This is just so much poppycock, however, as the Shermans knew just as well as the Eskimos that they were ordered into the finals." Calgary's protest came too late and the AAHA rejected it.

The Eskimos' Allan Cup challenge was accepted. Edmonton hockey fans were hopeful that their team's journey to Winnipeg would be fruitful, but their dreams of an amateur championship would soon be dashed. With a 9–6 win followed by a 9–2 thrashing of the Esks, the Victorias proved that maybe all of that Alberta controversy was for nothing, as that province's representatives were not of the same stuff as the defending champions.

The Big Four—"Shamateur" Hockey

By 1919, the Allan Cup had established itself as a major prize on the Canadian senior men's amateur hockey scene. While the Stanley Cup was reserved for pro teams, shutting out the majority of cities and leagues across Canada from the competition, the Allan Cup dream was alive in communities from coast to coast. As the Allan Cup continued to grow in popularity, the efforts of so-called "shamateur" teams to try and take the Cup intensified. Many of the teams tread a fine line between amateur and professional status. Nowhere was the line between pro and amateur more blurred than in the Big Four League, launched in 1919 with two teams each in Calgary and Edmonton. (The Big Four attempted to become the Big Five before the 1920–21 season. Discussions were held with Saskatoon, but league president Allan McCaw could not put a deal together to bring in the expansion club from Saskatchewan.)

The Edmonton Eskimos took the championship in 1919–20, thanks to the work of Gordon "Duke" Keats. The future Hockey Hall of Famer registered 47 points in 22 games to spur his team to the title. Those numbers were expected by Edmonton fans, as Keats had starred with the Toronto Blueshirts of the National Hockey Association—the forerunner of the National Hockey League—before defecting to the Western "amateur" ranks. There were nagging suspicions that Keats and a handful of other Big Four stars, including Eskimos stars "Bullet" Joe Simpson and Russell "Barney" Stanley (both would also later go to the Hall of Fame), were being paid under the table for their services, making the Big Four a pro league masquerading as an amateur circuit.

The 1920–21 campaign would see the title decided between the Eskimos, Edmonton Dominions, Calgary Canadians and Calgary Tigers. In fact, before the league reorganized for its second season, the Amateur Athletic Union of Canada decided that the league's amateur status should be revoked, a decision the Big Four tried to appeal. The Alberta Amateur Hockey Association tried to protect the Calgary and Edmonton Big Four teams by going on the offensive. Before the start of the 1920–21 season, AAHA president Frank Drayton appealed to the Canadian Hockey Association to investigate amateur hockey in Saskatchewan and Manitoba, claiming that the big clubs there were breaking the eligibility rules and entering illegal teams into the Allan Cup. As well, the Big Four teams alleged that the Winnipeg Falcons, the Canadian entry into the 1920 Olympics in Antwerp, Belgium, were getting money and should be treated as a professional team.

Drayton's accusations were splattered across the sports page of the *Edmonton Bulletin* just three days before the opening of the Big Four season on Christmas Day, 1920.

"President Drayton considers that the Alberta Association is the only one in Canada that is innocent of securing players wrongfully and that if a thorough investigation is held, it will be found that the Alberta Association is the only one in Canada with the possible exception of British Columbia that is qualified to play in the Allan Cup."[21]

Drayton should have muted his charges. The Edmonton Eskimos were not helping his claims that the Big Four should be recognized as amateurs. On the season opener, the Eskimos began their title defence in style. The Esks triumphed 4–2 over the Tigers in Calgary, and after the game both captain Keats and star defender Joe Simpson announced that the Eskimos were the best team in Canada— and better than any team the new National Hockey League could offer. In a time when the Esks should have kept the boasting down to continue the illusion that they really were an amateur team, they made headlines with their bring-'em-on bravado. "Duke Keats, captain and star center player, remarked that his lineup could beat anything in Canada, pro or amateur," read the *Bulletin*'s Boxing Day sports page.[22]

The Edmonton Dominions, unlike the Eskimos, flopped in their Christmas Day home opener at the Edmonton Arena. Powered by a hat trick from Red Dutton, the Calgary Canadians, who had been picked to be the stronger of the two Big Four teams from Calgary, decimated the Dominions by an 8–1 count.

The Canadians continued to fly high for their second game. With a 5–3 win over the Eskimos, the Canadians swept their two-game opening tour of Edmonton and cooled all of the hot air that had been coming from the Eskimos camp throughout the week. Eskimos captain Keats and Canadians star Dutton, both professional superstars before regaining their amateur status in Alberta, each had a goal and an assist. Over 3,500 fans packed the Edmonton Arena to see the game, with tickets costing 50 cents apiece.

The Eskimos funk did not continue; in fact, the team soon displayed the form that backed up Simpson and Keats's bluster and bravado. By the halfway mark of the season, the team had re-established itself as the favourite for the Big Four title. As Alberta celebrated hitting the half-million population mark, the Calgary Canadians played the ace up their sleeve in their attempt to halt the Eskimos' run at a second straight championship. They claimed that Bill Tobin, the Eskimos' netminder, had not lived in Alberta long enough to qualify for amateur status in the province.

The Eskimos vigorously defended Tobin, and McCaw ordered that the league halt play while the charges into Tobin were investigated. The Eskimos' appeal was successful and Tobin was deemed eligible, but both Calgary teams threatened to withdraw from the league if the Eskimos re-activated their goaltender. To placate the Calgarians, the Eskimos asked University of Alberta goaltender Slim Morris to take over in goal and offered to replay all games against the Calgary teams in which Tobin had appeared. Morris, however, wary of the league's poor standing, worried he would lose his amateur status by playing for the Eskimos, and he withdrew his services.

This series of events led an exasperated McCaw to cancel the championship. Even though the Eskimos and Tigers agreed to stage their own series to determine the league champion, McCaw refused to sanction such an event.

Frustrated by the president's inaction, Big Four vice-president Eddie Morris intervened and said he would support an Eskimos/Tigers series to decide who would be league champs. The two-game total-goals series would be called the Intercity Championship, and Tobin would be allowed to tend goal for the Eskimos.

Playing the game allowed the Tigers the chance to prove the Eskimos' early-season boasts wrong. With a 2–0 win at home, the Tigers gave themselves a large advantage. The Eskimos knew they would have to return home and win by two clear goals just to force a tiebreaker. Simpson and Keats were at their Hall-of-Fame best in the second game at the Edmonton Arena. Each man had a goal and an assist, but their efforts weren't enough to unseat the Tigers.

Future Hall of Famer Barney Stanley was a key part of the Tigers' win. He had been a star in the professional Pacific Coast Hockey Association before coming to the Big Four, and had won a title with Edmonton the year before. Tobin would survive the scandal and go on to coach, scout and eventually run the Chicago Black Hawks franchise in the 1940s after the death of team founder Major Frederic McLaughlin.

The Big Four was finished as a league. Both the Tigers and Eskimos would join the new Western Canada Hockey League in 1921–22. The WCHL would become Canada's third major professional hockey league—and the Eskimos and Tigers would continue their rivalry without any pretense of being amateurs.

Stanley Cup Fever in Alberta

During the early 1920s, pro hockey did better business than pretty well any other sport in North America outside of baseball. There was no major North American basketball league that would compete with hockey for gate money in the winter months, and football was still in its infancy.

Hockey players were, at the time, very well paid in comparison to their counterparts in other pro sports. The National Hockey League competed with the Patrick Family's western pro circuit, the Pacific Coast Hockey Association, to sign the best players in Canada. This created a great market for the players, who could play the two leagues off each other and ratchet up their contract demands.

Even though hockey was making the headlines on the sports pages in both Edmonton and Calgary, those same pages were evidence of just how close Alberta of the 1920s was to its British colonial roots. The hockey stories butted up against stories from the English and Scottish soccer leagues, and the *Bulletin* advertised a weekly football (as in soccer) pool where $121.25 in prize money was available to those who could pick the most winners over the next week's slate of English and Scottish football fixtures.

After the collapse of the "shamateur" Big Four League, the void of big-time hockey on the prairies was quickly filled by Canada's third official pro circuit. The Calgary Tigers and Edmonton Eskimos, refugees from the defunct Big Four circuit, agreed to become part of the Western Canada Hockey League, which would begin play in 1921 with the Regina Capitals and the Saskatoon Shieks. The new WCHL would continue to raise the stakes for hockey talent in North America. Now, mercenary players could play three leagues off each other. The new pro circuit on the prairies would also be allowed to compete for the Stanley Cup. At the end of the pro season, the champions from the WCHL, PCHA and NHL would be put into a mini-tournament out of which the Cup champ would emerge.

The early fortunes of the new league were poor as wages outstripped the gate receipts. Drowning in red ink, the Shieks left Saskatoon for Moose Jaw during the inaugural season and folded after the end of the campaign; the team would be replaced by the Saskatoon Crescents in season two.

As badly as the Tigers and Eskimos wanted the Allan Cup when they were "amateur" clubs in the Big Four league, once they became pro teams in the WCHL their desire for the Stanley Cup was much greater. At first, it looked like the Eskimos would be the team to beat. Thanks to the exploits of future Hall of Famers Gordon "Duke" Keats and "Bullet" Joe Simpson, the Eskimos finished the 1921–22 WCHL season with a berth in the final. Keats would score 31 times and add 24 assists over the course of the Eskimos' 25-game schedule, a pace of more than two points a game.

In terms of points-per-game production at a major professional level, Keats' numbers compare favourably with those of Wayne Gretzky during his halcyon days as an Oiler throughout the '80s. Bill Tobin was now officially a professional and starred between the pipes. "Artful Arthur" Gagne was the team's clutch-goal scorer, the man who would always find a way to pot a key goal when the game was on the line—the same role Glenn Anderson would assume with the Oilers in the '80s.

But the high-powered Esks were shocked by the Regina Caps in the final. The Esks lost the two-game total-goals series by a 3–2 count to a Caps team that featured the unflappable Bill Laird in goal and Dick Irvin as the on-ice catalyst. The same Dick Irvin would win 692 games as the head coach of the Chicago Black Hawks, Toronto Maple Leafs and Montreal Canadiens.

The Esks returned for the 1922–23 season with a vengeance. The team scored 113 goals over the 30-game WCHL schedule—best in the circuit—and topped the league with a 19–10–1 mark. They would be scheduled to match up with the Caps once again for the 1923 final, and they were out to avenge the 1922 upset.

The series opened in Regina. Two-game aggregate series were played in the following order: The first game was hosted by the team with the lesser record so the higher-ranked team could play the second game at home knowing how many goals were needed to cinch the series. The Esks fired 38 shots at the Caps' net. If not for Laird, the score would have been lopsided. But Gagne's lone goal was enough to give the Esks a slim margin heading home.

Game 2 would go down as one of the most thrilling

matches in Western Canadian hockey history. The Caps beat Esks goalie Hal Winkler three times; the Eskimos replied twice, leaving the series knotted at three goals apiece over the two games. The series would have to be decided in sudden death overtime—but the drama was spiked when Keats was awarded a penalty shot after Laird was adjudged to have interfered with an Eskimos' scoring opportunity. Keats and Laird faced off one-on-one to decide the series, and Keats and the Eskimos won, guaranteeing the team a trip to the Stanley Cup final.

"When the history of 1923 is written, the chroniclers, the savants and the learned men of letters may pass lightly over a certain epoch-making event that happened on the sixteenth day of the third month of that year..." wrote the *Edmonton Journal's* Fraser M. Gerrie the next day. "But seven thousand Edmonton citizens will tell their children and their children's children that it was on this night the Eskimos emblazoned their names large on the pages of hockey history by winning the championship of the Western Canada Hockey League in the most thrilling contest in the annals of the game in Western Canada."[23]

After taking the WCHL title, the Esks would be forced to wait out the result of the series between the PCHA champion Vancouver Maroons and the NHL champion Ottawa Senators. The Stanley Cup would be played as a tournament between the three Canadian major-league winners, all in the home arena of the PCHA champion Maroons. The Senators took the opening series three games to one, wrapping things up with a 5–1 thrashing of the Maroons on March 26. The Stanley Cup final, though, was scheduled to begin on March 29, which gave the Sens just three days to prepare to play the Eskimos, who had nearly two weeks to get to Vancouver and prepare for the winners of the NHL/PCHA series. Despite the break, Eskimos owner and general manager Kenny Mckenzie bemoaned the fact that his team could not find suitable ice in Vancouver on which to practice—and the Esks were only able to get one on-ice workout before the opening night of the series.

Despite the Senators having a power-packed lineup that boasted future Hall of Famers like Francis "King" Clancy, legendary goaltender Clint Benedict, and Cy Denneny, who had finished second to Babe Dye in the NHL scoring race that season with 23 goals and 11 helpers in 24 regular season games, pundits doubted they would win simply because of the fatigue factor. Injuries had also depleted the Senators so badly that manager Tommy Gorman feared that he might be able to use only six players for the series opener.

The bookmakers in Vancouver had made the Eskimos the favourite to win the Cup; Mckenzie, despite his team's lack of practice, declared they would win the best-of-three series in two straight. An electric scoreboard was installed at Mike's News Stand, the downtown Edmonton spot that served as the Eskimos' ticket agency, to display the results of the games in Vancouver as they happened.

If the Sens, exhausted from their series with the Maroons and three time zones away from home, were to beat the WCHL champs from Edmonton, they would have to use the guile that had won them Cups in 1920 and '21. Unfortunately for the Esks, that was exactly how the script unfolded. Benedict was the hero for the Senators in a 2–1 overtime win over Edmonton in Game 1; the Esks nursed a 1–0 lead going into the third, but Senators' defenceman Lionel Hitchman, who was not expected to play due to injury, tied the game with a shot that found its way through a maze of legs and past Esks' goalie Hal Winkler. Denneny won the game 2:08 into overtime, and the Esks were left scratching their heads, as they felt they had dominated the game.

"We had it on them like a tent. How we lost after all is still puzzling me. We were not over-confident and I think the game just ended proves that what confidence we had in our ability to outplay them was justified," wrote Simpson in a guest column in the *Edmonton Journal*.[24]

The Esks still felt they could win the next two games and take the series. But the Sens ended up proving Mckenzie right in the most ironic fashion. He had predicted a series sweep—and that's exactly what happened. Punch Broadbent beat Winkler from 40 feet out in the first period of Game 2; that would prove to be the only goal of the game. Benedict would not allow the high-powered Eskimos offence to get anything past him. If there was ever a playoff series where Benedict showed his Hall of Fame mettle, this was it.

The Esks went into the 1923–24 season confident they could return to the Stanley Cup final. They were wrong. The Eskimos went from league champs to the cellar, as they finished in last place in the four-team league. But the Tigers now took up the Alberta challenge for the province's first-ever Stanley Cup win. The Tigers finished the season with an 18–11–1 record, leaving them with 37 points out of 30 games, edging the Regina Capitals by one measly point for first-place overall in the WCHL regular season standings. Who came in first was moot; under the league playoff format at the time, the first- and second-place teams would be scheduled to clash in a two-game home-and-home total-goals championship.

The Caps featured future Hall of Famer Russell "Barney" Stanley, who had moved east to Saskatchewan in 1923, and the hard-nosed Irvin. Thanks to defenceman Herb Gardiner, who scored the opening goal and was named player of the game, the Tigers managed to get a 2–2 draw in Regina. The Caps had stormed back after trailing by two goals early on. The tie, though, was a good result for the Calgarians; all the Tigers would need was to win their home game to clinch the league and the right to play the Pacific Coast champs on their path to the Stanley Cup.

Game 2 was a bloody affair, a penalty-filled contest that saw the Tigers claim the championship with a 2–0 win. Charlie Reid got the shutout for the Tigers, but it was forward Cully Wilson who got most of the kudos for scoring the winning goal and then surviving an ugly stick-swinging incident with Irvin. With the Tigers already in the lead, both Wilson and Irvin were sent into the penalty box after they skirmished on the ice. But neither gave up the battle once they got to the sin bin. Both started swinging their sticks at each other's heads, and Irvin opened up a three-inch gash on Wilson's forehead.

"The blood came bubbling out through the yawning furrow down the right side of Wilson's head," read the *Calgary Herald* report the next day, "and although he was a gory-looking mess, the doctor's needle pulled the flesh together after the game, and Wilson is off to the coast with his mates to carry on the Stanley Cup series."[25]

Calgary went on to play the PCHA champion Vancouver

Maroons as part of a new PCHA/WCHL final, even though both were guaranteed berths in the Stanley Cup tournament. After dropping the first game in Vancouver, Calgary roared back with a 6–3 triumph at home and then a 3–1 win in the finale at Winnipeg. The Maroons then went to Montreal and were swept in best-of-three series by the Canadiens, giving the Habs the right to play the Tigers for the Cup.

The Canadiens' series with the Maroons gave the Tigers one full week to travel from Winnipeg to Montreal, but the Tigers fared even worse against the 1924 NHL champs than the Esks had fared a year before against the Senators. The Tigers' forwards were stymied by Canadiens' netminder Georges Vézina; the Tigers could only manage one goal in the Habs' two-game sweep, while the Montrealers tallied nine goals over the series. It was a humiliating blow for the WCHL, which had touted itself as a league that could rival the NHL. The size of the Canadiens' victory over the Tigers showed WCHL owners that they still had a ways to go before they could match the powerful circuit to the east.

By the next season, the PCHA found itself in dire straits. The Seattle Metropolitans, the first American franchise to ever hoist the Stanley Cup, folded, leaving the Pacific Coast pros with just two teams, the Victoria Cougars and Vancouver Maroons. A deal was forged with the WCHL to merge the two remaining teams into that league, but the added travel and the decline in crowds in the prairie cities put huge financial strains on the new WCHL during the 1924–25 season. The Cougars would save the face of Western Hockey by beating the Canadiens in the 1925 Stanley Cup final, but the WCHL was obviously in its final days. As the Stanley Cup was contested, Eskimos owner Kenny Mckenzie announced his intention to sell the team, which he claimed was bleeding money. That year, the Eskimos had been a major disappointment. Mckenzie had stretched the budget by re-signing Stanley, bringing one of the original Big Four Eskimos back to Edmonton. But Winkler had been inconsistent in goal, and eventually Mckenzie sold him to rival Calgary. "I am through with hockey, in this city, at least I have always tried to have a winning hockey team to represent Edmonton," said Mckenzie. "Paid real coin of the realm for all the players and I have never had a cheap club."[26]

The WCHL owners had set an example that modern NHL governors should have heeded. In an effort to prise top talent away from the likes of the Senators and the Canadiens, the WCHL had driven up salaries. In the mid-'20s, hockey players were among the highest-paid athletes in the world. Because there was no system in place to restrict player movement between the leagues, players could drive up their own prices and sell themselves to the highest bidder. Where a top pro baseball player could earn $5000 a year, hockey players could demand more.

The best example of this was Eddie Shore. Despite the Eskimos heavy financial losses (an estimated $10,000 after the 1924–25 season, a massive sum at that time), the team stretched itself even further in 1925–26 by bringing Shore, the highly touted Regina Caps defenceman, to Edmonton. Shore quickly earned the nickname "Edmonton Express" thanks to his take-no-prisoners, hard-hitting style. Shore's ability to lay out opponents with brute force made him the most-feared hockey player of his time. The Eskimos felt that Shore's ability to drill opponents would attract more fans to the Edmonton Arena and reverse their sagging financial fortunes.

Led by Keats and Shore, the Eskimos reached the WCHL final. A badly injured Shore played in the final against the Victoria Cougars, despite his leg bleeding so badly that blood pooled in his skate. Shore and the Eskimos fell short in their quest to beat the defending Cup champs from Victoria, the last non-NHL team to raise Lord Stanley's mug. The Cougars won the WCHL, but lost the Stanley Cup to the NHL champion Montreal Maroons.

The Tigers and Eskimos would both face new challenges when the WCHL folded after the 1925–26 season. The owners of the remaining WCHL teams made a deal with the NHL, worth an estimated $300,000. Shore and Keats were sent to the Bruins, where Shore was paid an astonishing $15,000 per year (at a time when Babe Ruth was receiving an estimated $10,000 per year). Tiger stars "Red" Dutton and Herb Gardiner went to the Canadiens, while their former teammates Archie Briden and Harry Oliver joined Shore and Keats in Beantown.

A new Prairie League was formed in the wake of the WCHL. Strictly a minor-pro circuit, it would give the new low-budget Tigers and Eskimos a home. Stanley returned to Edmonton, took over what was left of the Eskimos, and secured a deal to rent the arena in three instalments for a total of $2,500. But he only made the first $1,000 payment before defaulting. A group of 50 investors, led by local businessman John Michaels, temporarily saved the Esks, and urged fans to fill the seats (50 cents for cheap seats, 75 cents for premium tickets) in order to save the team.

The fans did not rally, and the 1926–27 season would be the Esks' last in the Prairie League. According to Edmonton City Council documents, the team reported a $7,755.12 loss in 1926–27. It carried expenses of $12,233.83, of which $6,005 were player salaries.

As the Eskimos struggled, the Tigers roared. The Calgarians took the regular season Prairie League title, and faced the Saskatoon Sheiks in the final. The series would be marred by controversy. After a 2–1 Tigers win in Game 1, the Sheiks went home angry with the refereeing of Harry Scott. Even though the league offered another referee, the deal was rejected and Calgary won the title by default. The Prairie League Champs would go on to play the reigning American Hockey Association champion Winnipeg Maroons for the Merchants Casualty Cup. Norman "Dutch" Gainor and Ernie Anderson scored for Calgary, enough to earn the Tigers a 2–1 win over the Maroons in Game 1 at the Victoria Arena. But Game 2 would never be played; the AHA ordered the Maroons to return to Winnipeg so they could compete in their own league, rather than play in a series that the league saw as nothing better than an exhibition. Calgary would win its second title in the space of two weeks by default.

The Prairie League, weighed down by the financial problems of all of its member teams, would soon fold, and professional hockey in Calgary and Edmonton would disappear.

But not for long. By the 1930s, new entrepreneurs and old legends would try to revive the Tigers/Esks rivalry.

Esks and Tigers—One Last Dance

The lessons of the free-spending '20s—and the collapse of professional hockey on the prairies because of owners who insisted on buying players they could not afford—did not fully sink in with hockey people in Edmonton and Calgary. In 1932, the Eskimos and Tigers were revived to become part of a new Western Canada Professional Hockey League. The timing could not have been worse. The prairies were in the throes of the Great Depression, and families simply didn't have the disposable income needed to support pro hockey. Fans who had once spent money watching the Tigers and Esks play were now on the unemployment rolls. In November of 1932, Calgary was swamped with transients when the city offered free bed and meal tickets to the unemployed.[27] The city, province and federal government split the nearly $1,000 a day it cost to run this program for over 2,000 men. Edmonton also had program to care for the jobless, with similar expenses.

Former Eskimos stars Gordon "Duke" Keats and "Artful Arthur" Gagne, who had both spent years in the NHL after the collapse of the original WCHL in 1926, returned for one more kick at the can with the new Eskimos. Lloyd Turner, the man who had steered the Tigers since their Big Four days, returned with a bang. In a move to try and get hometown fans to jump on the bandwagon and buy tickets in advance of the inaugural 1932–33 campaign, he signed Bill Hutton, who had previously spent three years in the NHL with Boston, Ottawa and Detroit. Hutton, being a Calgarian, was pegged to be the hometown hero of the new squad. Kenny Mckenzie, the man who bankrolled and then bailed out on the Eskimos during their first stab at pro hockey, returned as the financier of the revamped Regina Caps.

The Eskimos opened the season at the Edmonton Arena with a 1–0 win over the Tigers. The shutout came courtesy of Earl Robertson, who had been signed by the Calgary Tigers but was traded to Edmonton before the start of the season. The attendance numbers for the home opener foreshadowed the woe the new league would have to endure. Barely over 2,000 fans showed up to watch the game, far less than would have paid to see the Eskimos match-up with their rival Tigers in the '20s.

The playoff format for the new league was simple: The team that finished first overall would go directly to the championship series, the second- and third-place finishers would play off against each other for the right to play the regular season leader for the 1933 WCHL championship. The Tigers topped the league and earned a berth in the WCHL final. The Eskimos, thanks to a late-season eight-game win streak in which Robertson reeled off four straight shutouts, had to face the Vancouver Maroons for the right to play the Tigers. Thanks to the stellar play of Robertson, the Esks upset Vancouver, setting up an all-Alberta final.

Robertson, from Bengough, Saskatchewan, would eventually make his way to the NHL with a six-game run with the Red Wings in the 1937 playoffs. His performance got the attention of GMs around the NHL, and he was signed by the New York Americans in the 1937 off-season; he would play with the team until it folded during the Second World War.

The first game, held at Victoria Arena, was played in sloppy, slushy conditions. As there was no artificial refrigeration at the Calgary rink, the play suffered thanks to some warm spring weather. Gagne, well into his 30s, showed that he could still be the Eskimos' clutch player, as his goal secured a 1–1 tie after regulation. The two teams played three overtime periods and could not decide a winner; after the third extra frame, the ice got to the point where it was unplayable, and a tie was declared. Because of the poor playing conditions, the WCHL ordered that the remaining playoff games be played at the Edmonton Arena. The Eskimos, who had barely got into the playoffs, now enjoyed unfettered home ice advantage thanks to...what else? The weather!

But the ice in Edmonton was only marginally better. Robertson and Calgary Tigers' goaltender Red McCusker duelled to a 1–1 draw in Game 2. It was called after just one period of overtime because of the excess water on the playing surface. The crowds had improved—3,500 had come to see the game, but that was still less than the senior amateur Superiors got for their Alberta finals games against the Calgary Bronks.

A cold snap helped the playing conditions for Game 3. Art Townsend assisted on the Esks first goal and scored the winner as the Edmontonians won by a 2–1 count. The Tigers thought they had tied the score late on a goal by Johnny Houbreggs, but the referee ruled that a Tiger had interfered with Robertson in the crease. With that win, Edmontonians turned on to their pro team. Over 6,000 fans came to the Arena for Game 4, setting a new attendance record for the building. Even though the game faced off at 9 p.m. (so the cooler night temperatures could help keep the ice in good playing shape), Edmontonians jammed the rink like they had never done all season long. Robertson was once again the hero; he shut out the Tigers in a 2–0 Eskimos win and established himself as the most important player in the series. The win put the Eskimos within one game of clinching the series.

Despite the efforts of the league and the Eskimos, bad ice plagued the game. League president E.L. Robertson knew that spring was near, and that the series needed to end as quickly as possible. He ordered that there be no more off-days. Game 5 would be played March 27; Game 6 on March 28; and, if needed, Game 7 would go March 29. The Eskimos could not repeat their domination performance in Game 5. The Tigers' slumping offence finally woke up, and they thrashed the "Igloo-Men" (a favourite nickname for the Eskimos) by a 5–1 count.

Edmonton entered Game 6 poised to stage a major upset, and Gagne made sure that they did. His first period goal was the Esks' lone marker in a 1–1 tie over three periods. Unlike Games 1 and 2, though, this match did not end in a tie. Gagne took a pass from Keats and scored at 8:30 of the first overtime period. The goal allowed Edmontonians to celebrate for one last time the greatest goal-scoring combination their city had seen to this point. Gagne from Keats— like watching Jari Kurri bury a pass from Gretzky for one last time. "It was an exceptionally brilliant display of the ice sport that was provided as the two teams fought in the all-important battle," read the sports page in the *Edmonton Bulletin* the next day. "In fact, one of the finest games of hockey the old Arena has produced this winter."[28]

The upset infuriated Turner and his Tigers, and they vowed to gain revenge on the Esks and take the Northwestern League title in 1934—the circuit was renamed before the 1933–34 campaign when the Saskatchewan clubs dropped out of competition. A little over 4,000 Edmonton fans got a preview of things to come on opening night of the season. The visiting Tigers pasted the Eskimos by an 8–5 count, and the score was flattering to the Esks, as they scored four third-period goals after the game was well out of reach.

"Without having seen what Portland, Seattle or Vancouver have to offer, I'd say the Tigers are the class of the loop, and that they'll set the pace right down the line if they've a mind to and if they keep clear of injuries. They have balance in every division, and they sure had no lead in their shoes when they were running wild in the middle frame of Saturday's game."[29] The hungry Tigers proved the *Herald* pundit right and stormed to the top of the league. Meanwhile, the Eskimos struggled and soon Keats was swimming in a sea of red ink due to declining gate receipts. By March, the Eskimos surged and got into a dogfight with the Vancouver Lions and the Tigers for first place. When the season ended, the Esks and Tigers both finished the season with 40 points, but the Tigers' +41 goal difference (compared to Edmonton's +7) gave the Calgarians first place and forced the Eskimos into a preliminary series playoff with the Lions, who finished five points back of the leaders. The playoff system of the time dictated that the first place team got a bye into the final, while the second and third place teams had to face off in a best-of-three preliminary playoff series.

The Eskimos should have had two home games in the best-of-three series. However, because the Esks did not have artificial ice, the league ordered that Game 1 be played in Vancouver and Game 2 in Seattle, where both had artificial icemaking. The road trip hurt the Esks, who were swept by 4–3 and 3–1 scores. These scores would have been more lopsided had it not been for Robertson, who was swamped by Lions shots.

The Tigers were then ordered to head west. Despite finishing in first overall, they would have to contest the entire final series away from the Victoria Arena (in Calgary) so there would be no danger of their home games being disrupted by the spring weather. Calgary played their first "home" in Seattle. Despite losing several teeth thanks to a hard check early in the first period, Norman "Dutch" Gainor, the Northwestern League's leading scorer, paced the Tigers to a 6–2 win in Game 1 with a two-goal effort.

The scene shifted from Seattle to Vancouver for the remainder of the series. The Lions roared with a 7–2 win in the second game, but Louis Coupez was the star of the Tigers' 3–2 Game 3 triumph. Coupez registered a goal and two assists that put Calgary within one game of clinching the title. The Lions tied the series with a 2–1 win, setting up a winner-take-all deciding game. The final should have been Calgary's home game; instead, over 6,000 Vancouver fans jammed their home arena, cheering for the Lions to pull off the upset. Their dreams were crushed as the Tigers trounced the Lions by a 6–1 count. Early goals from Tip O'Neill and Hutton would set the stage for the rout.

The final game only made it to second page of the *Calgary Herald*'s sport pages. In the minds of Calgarians, the Northwestern League was a poor substitute for the NHL, which dominated the front page of the sports section. An NHL playoff series between the Red Wings and Maple Leafs got more space than the hometown heroes. In the days of the old Western Canada Hockey League, there was no way the Tigers would have been knocked off the front page of the sports section.

Fan apathy as well as the growth of the Depression put the Northwest League in a terrible position. By the fall of 1934, the Edmonton Military Institute had begun collecting housewares, clothing, books and other goods for distribution to the unemployed men who had gathered in relief camps. This was not a time to be thinking about season tickets or playoff races; this was a time to wonder how on Earth a man could make enough to feed his family.

The hardheaded businessmen who ran the Northwest circuit voted to keep the league going for the 1934–35 season, with both the Esks and Tigers still key parts. Just two weeks into the season, however, the league was forced to hold an emergency meeting as the Eskimos teetered on the brink of financial collapse. The team started the season with eight straight losses. The Esks installed the legendary Gagne in the coach's spot to try and stop the bleeding.

Calgary could not repeat the form of the previous season. The Eskimos crisis weighed heavily on the Tigers. If the Eskimos folded, the Tigers would be an isolated team in the mountain time zone while the rest of the league played on the Pacific coast. The Tigers and Eskimos both missed the playoffs, and both soon slipped into obscurity. As both teams attracted very little media attention by the mid-'30s, their exit from the world of pro hockey was not followed by glowing epitaphs from the sportswriters. They were once champions, then widely ignored, then gone.

In 1943, Keats and the Eskimos made one more headline. After the 1933 WCHL win, the Eskimos were awarded the Merchants' Casualty Cup. After the season, Keats had sent it to a silversmith for repairs, and then with all the confusion over his ownership duties and the switch of leagues, he had forgotten it there. It would remain lost for 10 years until it was found by an Edmonton reporter in a hock-shop window, with a tag saying that any offer would be accepted for the mysterious prize.

The Goal That Didn't Count

The onset of the Great Depression was one of the two major factors that prevented the revamped Calgary Tigers and Edmonton Eskimos from being financial successes in the early '30s, the other factor being the fans' preference for senior amateur hockey. Families simply didn't have the disposable income to fritter away on pro hockey tickets. Those that did have money hoarded it, fearing that they too could join the ranks of the jobless. While pro hockey did not succeed, Albertans had not lost their passion for the game. Both the Edmonton Superiors and Calgary Bronks, two of the top senior amateur teams in the West, played to full houses in their respective cities. Fans were willing to support the more affordable amateur games, and the success of these two clubs was the second major factor in the downfall of Esks and Tigers. The pro teams could not knock the amateurs off the front of the sports pages.

In the early '30s, the Superiors, bankrolled by the Gainer's meat packing operation, asserted themselves as the top amateur program in the province. Ironically, Gainer's would continue to be associated with hockey until towards the end of the century. The meat packer was eventually purchased by Peter Pocklington, who owned the Oilers at the same time. The most notable player on that Superiors team was James "Buster" Brown, who won Commonwealth Games gold in 1930 as part of the Canadian 4x100 relay team and won the Bennett Cup, which went to Alberta's top track athlete, three times. As well, he was one heck of a hockey player.

The "Soops," as they were affectionately known, had captured the Herald-Journal Cup as senior provincial champions in 1931. But Ira Stuart's team could not rest on their laurels. The Bronks quickly asserted themselves as the top team in the southern half of the province at the outset of the 1931–32 season propelled by Dave "Sweeney" Schriner, who would later be inducted into the Hockey Hall of Fame after a stellar career with the New York Americans and Toronto Maple Leafs. It can still be easily argued that Schriner was the best hockey player this province had produced during the first half of the 20th century.

No one was shocked when the two teams faced each other for the provincial title, with the winner advancing in the Western Canada playdowns for the Allan Cup. Really, the Bronks and Soops had been on a collision course the whole season. As defending champions, the Superiors were favoured to take the best-of-three series, even though the final would open in Calgary's Victoria Arena. But the Superiors were defeated by the Bronks' defensive game; slushy ice conditions made sure that the Soops' quick-passing attack would be neutralized, and if the Edmonton boys got anywhere close to the net, Bronks' netminder DeePee

McDonald was more than equal to the task. A 2–0 win on home ice was the deserved result for the Bronks.

Even though the Soops lost the opener, they were confident they could square the series at home. Over 6,000 fans backed up that claim, jamming the Edmonton Arena, despite the fact the mercury had plummeted to -15°C (-5° F). The indoor rink would be warmed by the heat generated by the fans, but it was still an awfully cold game to sit through. What unfolded was maybe the most controversial game ever to be played between the two cities.

Early goals from Schriner and Alex Luft, his linemate, gave the Bronks a shocking 2–0 lead, but the Soops turned up the pressure in the second period as they tried to scratch and claw their way back into the series—and prove that McDonald could be beaten in the Bronks' goal. A Soops shot came through a maze of players in front of McDonald. The shot hit McDonald in the pad, but the momentum of the shot carried it past the Bronks' netminder. The puck trickled towards the goal line. Those in the Arena roared when the goal judge, seated behind the Bronks' goal, waved his hand in the air to signal a goal. Immediately, McDonald skated to head referee Ken Paul, claiming that he had placed his pad over the puck, freezing it before it had totally crossed the line. As the entire puck had to cross the line for the goal to stand, McDonald claimed that the Soops were inches away from getting their first goal of the series, but had fallen short. Paul, convinced by McDonald's argument, asked the goal judge to come onto the ice—to actually place the puck on the spot where he last had clear view of it. The goal judge placed it right on the goal line, and admitted he had been hasty to call a goal.

Paul waved off the goal, setting off a bizarre chain of events. After Paul disallowed the Soops' claims for the goal, he was confronted by not only the entire Edmonton team, but by his assistant referee, Clarence Campbell, who after the Second World War would become the most storied president in the history of the National Hockey League. Campbell insisted that the goal should count. When Soops' coach Ira Stuart left the bench to confront Paul on the ice, all hell threatened to break loose.

"Finally, after he had waited for some time, during which, incidentally, the players of both teams argued the point vehemently and came dangerously near blows, the referee decided that it should not count and went to face off the puck at the side of the goal. Manager Stuart, of the Superiors, came on the ice to seek an explanation but was banished and the puck was faced off by Paul, with the goal not counting."[30]

As the protests raged on the ice, the 6,000-plus fans who had braved the cold temperatures and jammed the Edmonton Arena demonstrated their displeasure with the officiating. "Fans also took a part in the proceedings by hurling chairs on the ice, which again delayed the game as Referee Paul made several attempts to face the puck," read the *Calgary Herald* the next day.[31] To try and restore order, Alberta Amateur Hockey Association president W.G. Hardy, an Edmontonian, came to ice level and made a deal with Stuart and the Superiors. He promised that if the disallowed goal would have had any bearing on the result of the game, he would entertain a formal protest from Edmonton. When the Soops' Bob Crossland scored late in the third to make it 2–1, the Superiors knew they had a case. If the goal had counted, the score would have been tied and the result would have been in doubt. After the game, Hardy accepted their protest, with Calgary-based observers looking on in dismay.

Any conspiracy theorist would love to go through the game report of the 1932 provincial senior championship. Not only did assistant referee Campbell insist that the Soops' claimed goal should count, he also disallowed three Bronks goals. "If the game is not allowed to stand and is thrown out by the Alberta Hockey Association, it will be one of the most unfair decisions ever arrived at in the history of sport in this province," cried the *Calgary Herald*.[32] "The Bronks lost three goals through the decisions of Clarence Campbell, assistant referee, and when the Superiors lose one as a result of Ken Paul's ruling there's a protest. If that is sportsmanship then we don't know what the word means."

Needless to say, the *Edmonton Bulletin*'s Bill Lewis disagreed with the *Herald*'s take on the protest. "I have never heard of a protest which had better grounds behind it, and it would be the greatest mistake the AAHA ever made if the protest was thrown out." [33]

The AAHA promised to deliver swift justice. The executive would vote via telegraph whether to back the Superiors' claim that Game 2 be replayed. Two days after the controversial game, on March 3, 1932, the AAHA voted to deny the Superiors' claims and awarded the provincial championship to the Bronks. The AAHA executive claimed that it was powerless to overturn a Canadian Amateur Hockey Association rule which clearly stated that the referee has the right to overrule a goal at any time during the game, and that decision cannot be overturned—even by an executive council. They agreed that Paul's verdict must be treated as hockey gospel, simply to protect the integrity of the game and the CAHA.

Even though the Bronks took the Alberta title (but did not get to the Allan Cup final), the Superiors, thanks to Gainer's money, continued to enjoy a higher profile than their Calgary rivals in Western Canada. The team accepted an invitation to barnstorm Europe and to participate in the 1933 International Championships, held in St. Moritz, Switzerland. The Superiors played in front of 14,000 fans in an outdoor game in Paris and won the tournament in Switzerland—after months of travel through Europe, the team arrived back in Edmonton in time to try and gain revenge on Schriner and those darned Bronks in the 1933 final.

Schriner was actually the goat in the first game of the series, even though he scored a goal and added an assist. Over 4,000 fans jammed Calgary's Victoria Arena to watch a thrilling 2–2 tie pushed into overtime, but were shocked when Schriner, the team's top player, allowed the Soops' Joe Brown to strip him of the puck right in front of the Bronks goal. Brown slammed the puck past Bronks' goaltender McDonald to give the Soops the edge in the best-of-three final.

The Superiors won the deciding game 4–3 in overtime, but the truth is that they outplayed the Bronks for 58 of 60 minutes. The championship game saw the Superiors march into the last minute of regulation time with a 3–1 lead, and then Soops coach Stuart broke a cardinal rule of the sport—he rubbed the score in his opponents faces before the final horn had sounded. With a couple of minutes left, he allowed his entire first line to leave the bench and head to the dressing room so they could begin their celebrations early. The Bronks, incensed by this act of counting chickens before they hatch, sent Schriner and his line out onto the ice searching for a miracle. Fuelled by the arrogance of the Soops, Schriner scored with 20 seconds left on the clock. Just 15 seconds later, Bronk Red Creighton beat Soops' netminder Don Stuart to tie the game. There were just five seconds left in regulation. The Soops had blown a game which they had dominated. But Pal Power gave the Soops the win in the second overtime period. At that time, the Alberta Amateur Hockey Association did not sanction sudden death overtime, so the Superiors had to stave off Calgary attack after Calgary attack until time expired in the second overtime frame.

Like the Bronks the season before, the Soops' Allan Cup challenge did not get far past the provincial championship stage. But these two teams were the top draws in their respective cities—and would pave the way for even more senior-amateur hockey mania after the end of the Second World War.

Living Here in Allantown

The end of the Second World War ushered in a new era in Alberta. Not only was there a general feeling of euphoria that comes when a major conflict ends, but in 1947 oil was struck in Leduc. By the end of the '40s, the oil boom was well underway, transforming Alberta from an agriculture-first province into the strongest economic power in Canada. By 1948, the farming industry would post $347 million in total revenue, the highest in the province's history to that point.

In the era of the oil strike, the Calgary Stampeders and Edmonton Flyers each claimed the Allan Cup and helped establish Alberta as a hockey power on a national level. Not until these teams won Allan Cups did the hockey powers east of Winnipeg recognize that Alberta would soon compete with them as one of the top talent-producing regions in the country.

For decades after the Allan Cup was created, it generated national headlines. It was not the Stanley Cup, but in terms of prestige, it was awfully close. In the first post-war hockey season (1945–46), the Calgary Stampeders and

Edmonton Flyers emerged as hockey powers in the new Western Canadian Senior Hockey League. Both cities had a simple goal: to be the first Alberta city to toast an Allan Cup victory. However, no team could claim home ice advantage in the Allan Cup—the games were awarded to rinks across Canada, which also enhanced the competition's popularity.

The Stampeders quickly established themselves as a powerhouse. The team finished the 1945–46 WCSHL season with an average of over six goals per game. Dunc Grant, who would play with the Stamps until 1951, led the way with 45 goals, and during the season enjoyed a career night scoring five times in one period. Ken "Red" Hunter finished the 36-game season with a whopping 81 points, a new record for senior amateur hockey. The Stamps' scoring leader was pushed by Flyers sniper Bob Carse, who finished the season with 78 points. Calgary finished atop the standings with a 28–7–1 record. The Stamps' first-place finish guaranteed them a spot in the WCSHL final, where they would face the winner of the semifinal series between the Flyers and the Saskatoon Elks. The Flyers were heavily favoured, having finished the season 24–10–2, and they didn't disappoint—it was a relatively easy three-game sweep.

A Flyers/Stamps final made for hockey theatre at its best. The two teams had played each other 12 times during the regular season schedule; each had won six of those encounters. What made their season series so interesting is that, in their six wins, Edmonton had outscored Calgary by a 31–19 count; in their six wins, the Stamps had outscored the Flyers by a 45–18 margin. Despite the fact that they sawed off the 12 games, those matches themselves were not close games, as the goal tallies show. If the regular season form held true, fans could indeed expect a seven-game series, with each game decided before the second intermission.

The series opened at Calgary's Victoria Arena, and Grant would show that his better-than-one-goal-per-game scoring pace during the season would continue into the playoffs. His hat trick paced the Stamps to an easy 6–1 blowout win. This pattern was followed in Game 2. This time, it was the less-heralded Bunny Dame with the hat trick, as the Stamps skated to a 6–2 win. With the move north to Edmonton for Games 3 and 4, it would have been easy for the handicapper to guess that it would be the Flyers now handing out the shellackings. A sell-out crowd of 6,500 jammed the Edmonton Gardens in hopes of seeing their team turn the series around. But Grant decided to throw the form book out the window. Instead of capitulating to Edmonton, the Stamps took a commanding 3–0 lead in the series with a 3–2 triumph. Grant posted two goals, and had a third disallowed.

Ken McAuley played a strong game in net for the Flyers in Game 4, leading them to a 3–2 win to avoid the sweep, but there was no avoiding the feeling that the series would soon be coming to a close. In what has to be considered an anticlimactic finish, the Stamps stomped the Flyers on home ice by a 5–0 count, with Calgary goaltender Russ Dertell—who had earlier been named the top goalie in the WCSHL—getting the shutout.

The WCSHL championship put the Stampeders in the Western playdowns for the Allan Cup. Their first task was to beat the Winnipeg Orioles, who had already made Calgary fans angry before the series began. Orioles coach Stan Evans predicted it would take his Orioles squad only the minimum three games to oust the Stamps. After the Stamps took the first game by a 5–1 count, Stamps fans were thinking that Evans was half right, that the series would indeed end in a sweep, but with Calgary moving on, not Winnipeg.

"The inference was there—Winnipeg would win three straight to dash Calgary's fondest hopes of seeing an Allan Cup final...," wrote *Calgary Herald* sports editor Bob Mamini,[34] "and Stampeders supporters saw the 5–1 victory at Saskatoon as the handwriting on the wall. Stampeders would win three straight." Those Stamps fans were right. The Calgarians drilled the Orioles by 10–2 and 8–2 counts in the next two games.

After disposing of the Orioles, the Stamps had to take on the famous Trail Smoke Eaters, who had won gold at the 1939 World Championships, for the Western Canadian title and the right to play the Eastern champ for the Allan Cup. The Smoke Eaters were considered Canada's elite senior amateur team of the era, and by beating them, the Stamps earned a major confidence-booster going into the final. It wasn't easy. After the teams tied 1–1 in Game 1 on the tiny ice surface in Kootenay (ties were allowed in the playoffs at the time; the winner would be the first team to eight points, with two points awarded for a win, and one point each in the event of a tie), the Stamps needed a goal from Doug Cairns to tie Game 2 at 4–4 in front of a disgruntled home crowd at the Victoria Arena. Cairns would upstage Grant and Henry as the hero of the Western final; he would score two goals and add two assists in Calgary's 7–3 Game 3 victory, and would score two more in the Game 5 clincher that the Stamps took by a 4–2 count.

As the best team in the West, the Stamps earned the right to face the Eastern champion Hamilton Tigers in the best-of-seven Allan Cup final. There were worries that the Hamilton players would forego the Allan Cup, slated to be played in the West, because the $6 per day the team paid them was not enough to justify the vacation time needed from their jobs. But an eleventh-hour agreement was reached and the Hamiltonians made the trip west.

The final series would not only see the Stamps become the first Alberta team to win the Allan Cup, but they got the chance to kick Edmonton fans in the teeth. The final series was rotated throughout the West, and, with Calgary leading the series three games to one, Game 5 was scheduled for the Edmonton Gardens. The Stamps, famous for their offensive skill, put on a stifling defensive display. Goalie Russ Dertell was the star as the Stamps won 1–0. A spectacular 45-foot effort from Archie Wilder—who had played 18 games with the Detroit Red Wings as a wartime replacement player—was all the offence that the Stamps would need. The Edmonton Gardens faithful, nearly 6,000 strong, had to watch the Stampeders parade the Allan Cup on the Flyers' home ice.

"It was a variety of the same team play with which Stampeders chalked up 42 victories this season," read the *Calgary Herald* the next day. "It was the team play which had only permitted nine defeats in the 56 games played. And it was only a 'variety' of that team play because a club that has specialized on offence suddenly found itself in a position where everything depended on protecting a one-goal lead. The team's defensive effort found every man playing his position, and playing it well, to make it a glorious windup to a strenuous season which began six and a half months ago."[35]

Dave "Sweeney" Schriner, the Calgary-bred star who had just retired from the NHL and would later go on to the Hall of Fame, said the Allan Cup win was a major historical moment in his hometown's history. "One of the greatest things that ever happened. It'll boost Calgary as a sports city, and it has been quite a sports city all along."[36]

Thousands of fans greeted the Stamps as they arrived in Calgary with the Allan Cup. Stamps coach Jack Arbour told the crowd that he thought that the team's toughest challenge of all came in that WCSHL final against the Flyers. "If Stampeders hadn't won the Allan Cup, I'm sure Edmonton would have taken it."[37]

Ron "Squeak" Leopold, who would later go on to to become one of the top scorers in Stampeders history, recalls watching those old Stamps teams of the '40s. "I was a rink rat, and I remember watching those guys, Archie Wilder, Bob Brownridge. I lived close to the old Victoria Arena and I used to sneak in. A lot of us would end up scraping the ice after the game was done and we got a chance to play after it was flooded. Sometimes it was in our skates, sometimes it was in our feet with a tennis ball."

The Stamps stormed to another Western Canadian championship in 1947, and were pitted in the Allan Cup final against the powerful Montreal Royals, who featured future Hall of Fame defenceman Doug Harvey and Gerry McNeil in net, both of whom would later play for the Montreal Canadiens. The Stamps were beaten, with the deciding game played in front of over 11,000 fans in Quebec.

With Calgary winning the Allan Cup in 1946 and taking

the WCSHL championship again in 1947, Edmonton fans demanded that the Flyers step up and take bragging rights away from their Alberta rivals. But the Flyers would need more help to meet this challenge. They entered the 1947–48 season with an ace in the hole; Saskatchewan native Al Rollins, who had tended goal for the Vancouver Canucks the previous season, had been signed to help the Flyers in their push for the Cup.

Rollins was heavily scouted by NHL teams. Unlike most of his teammates, who had settled into senior amateur hockey as their lot in lives, the 21-year-old goalie was using his time with the Flyers as a stepping stone to the NHL. He would go on to an outstanding NHL career that saw him win a Stanley Cup and a Vezina Trophy with the 1950–51 Toronto Maple Leafs, and the Hart Trophy as the NHL's most valuable player in 1954 as a member of the Chicago Black Hawks. Ironically, when his career was on the downswing, he would face the Flyers as a member of the Calgary Stampeders, after the team became Chicago's farm club.

During the 1947–48 regular season, the Flyers didn't have the stuff to knock the Stampeders off their WCSHL perch. They finished the season with a 24–22–2 mark, good enough for only third place in the league, well behind the first-place Stamps and the second-place Regina Caps. The fact that they lost their season opener by a 4–2 count to Calgary did nothing to boost the hopes of Flyers supporters. But there were some signs of hope in what was really nothing much more than a mediocre regular season. Forwards Morey Rimstad and Andy Clovechok helped the Flyers score 231 regular season goals (an average of almost five a game!), the most in the league. Rimstad finished the season with 80 points in 48 games, while Clovechok scored 35 times.

Rollins posted a 24–20–2 regular season mark with a 3.20 goals-against average. Those weren't heady numbers, but Rollins would more than prove his worth in the play-offs, where he would put on a playoff run comparable to that of other future Edmonton goaltending legends Glenn Hall and Grant Fuhr.

The Flyers met the Caps in the first round of the play-offs, while the Stamps faced the fourth-place Lethbridge Maple Leafs. After splitting the first two games of the best-of-five series in Regina, the Flyers made the most of home ice in Games 3 and 4. The Caps stormed out to a 4–1 lead in Game 3 at the Edmonton Arena, but the Flyers rallied with four unanswered goals to take the series lead. In Game 4, Clovechok was the hero, scoring four times in a 5–3 win—giving the Flyers the upset triumph. Meanwhile, the Stampeders were taken to the maximum five games by the Maple Leafs. If the Stamps hadn't recovered from a 5–1 Game 3 deficit to win 7–5, the lacklustre Calgarians would have been upset. But with a 7–2 triumph in the fifth and deciding game, the Stamps avoided embarrassment. Being extended to five games in their first-round series would haunt the Stamps. The WCSHL final was scheduled to start the next night at Calgary's Victoria Arena, so the Stamps would have to renew their rivalry with the Flyers without one single day of rest.

As the Flyers and Stamps got set to decide the Western Canadian title, the game of hockey was in its darkest period since the end of the Second World War. The National Hockey League had just been rocked by a gambling scandal uncovered by Detroit police. A number of NHLers had been in contact with known Detroit-based gamblers and racketeers. When the dust settled, Rangers star Billy "The Kid" Taylor—a former Maple Leafs and Red Wings great—was banned for life after admitting to NHL president Clarence Campbell that he had placed a bet on a Black Hawks/Bruins game. To add insult to injury, Taylor had actually lost that bet.

The Canadian Amateur Hockey Association met at the same time to discuss the future of the Allan Cup. A faction within the CAHA had called for the Allan Cup to be taken away from the amateurs, as teams like the Flyers and Stampeders (really, examples were popping up across the nation) were stocking up with former pros—and players who should be pros—and calling them amateurs. After a controversial vote, the CAHA decided to keep the Allan Cup as it was, but the discussions would put continued pressure on teams like the Quebec Aces, Trail Smoke Eaters and the Eskimos and Flyers to declare whether or not they were truly professional clubs. Within three years, both the Calgary and Edmonton teams would join the Pacific Coast minor-pro circuit and officially declare themselves pro clubs.

The Stamps sure didn't look like they were suffering from the lack of rest in Game 1 of the WCSHL final. Stan Devicq, a former Flyer and an Edmonton native, stuck a stick blade through the heart of his former club with two goals and an assist as the Stamps went on to a 4–0 whitewash. But Rollins would steal Game 2. He was undoubtedly the star of a 3–2 win, and Flyers fans smelled an upset was in the making. The series moved north to Edmonton, but the Flyers stumbled on home ice. The Stamps looked good for a 3–2 win, but Flyer Bing Merluk tied it at 3–3 with a late third-period goal, after Clovechok had scored two for the Flyers. Rimstad had been the regular season star, but the Flyers were getting contributions from throughout the lineup to make up for the WCSHL scoring leader's lack of playoff production. Overtime settled nothing. The game was declared a 3–3 tie, normal playoff procedure at the time. The final series format was not a straight best-of-seven series; the winner was the first team to get to eight points. After three games, both Calgary and Edmonton had three points apiece, thanks to a win and a tie each.

Merluk was the star of Game 4 as well. His two goals helped the Flyers to a narrow 6–5 triumph over the Stamps. The Flyers had actually led the game by a 6–2 count, but a furious comeback by the Stamps had Edmonton fans biting their fingernails as the seconds ticked down in the third period. "If the Flyers wanted to throw a scare into their loyal rooters, they couldn't have gone about it better than they did at the Arena Saturday night," wrote *Edmonton Journal* sports editor George Mackintosh the next day.[38] "They came as close to tossing a win into the ash can as you're likely to see." After four games, the series was as pressure packed as Leduc #1, the oil well that had blown out of control during the WCSHL final and spewed roughly 200 barrels worth of oil into the air every hour until crews capped it.

Merluk, the offensive MVP of the series, struck again in Game 5, a game that Calgary needed to have at home. Merluk scored twice in a 4–2 Edmonton win. That road victory took all the air out of the Stamps' balloon. The

Stampeders offered little resistance in Game 6, going down to a 6–2 loss. Finally, in their third try, the Flyers had vanquished the Stamps, even though the playoff win defied the poor form the team had shown during the regular season.

Even though their teams were bitter enemies, Calgarians and Edmontonians shared one viewpoint—that the WCSHL was the best senior amateur league in the West. Once the league champion was decided, they both knew that team would be favoured to make it through the Western Allan Cup playdowns. The Flyers would not fail that challenge. They swept the Trail Smoke Eaters in their next series, with the Edmontonians registering a whopping 10–0 win in the deciding game. The Winnipeg Red Flyers (also knows as the Reos) were the next victims on the list. While the Winnipeggers did manage to win one game in the best-of-five series, they really were never close. The Flyers outscored Winnipeg by a 29–11 margin over the five games. The city's hockey fans were in a frenzy—the Flyers were just one series away from evening the score with those dreaded Stampeders.

Frank Roggeveen, who went on to play for the Flyers from '55–'59, after the franchise had become the farm team of the Detroit Red Wings, remembers how he and future Flyers teammates used to try and get into the Edmonton Gardens to see as many of the amateur Flyers games as possible.

"Norm Ullman, Lionel Repka and myself used to be able to get standing-room tickets for I think about a buck. But the place was so full all the time that we would have been able to turn around and sell those tickets for two dollars apiece! I remember that there were a few times we would go up the construction work, and we watched a few games right from the rafters!

"The games were really interesting to watch—not like now, I don't even watch hockey anymore. Back then you used to see skill and great one-one battles. Now, the game is all about chasing the puck and trying to hammer the other team. I think they made those changes for the Yankees, who don't care about our game in the first place!"

The Allan Cup championship series pitted the Flyers against the Eastern champion Ottawa Senators, who had come from behind to take out the Hamilton Tigers in their last series. The Senators required an extra Game 8 to beat the Tigers, so they would face the same exhaustion problem that the Stamps had faced in the WCSHL final. The best-of-seven final would see games played across the West. Game 1 faced off in Regina, and the Flyers won by a 6–2 count. With heavy flooding across the prairies due to unusually warm spring temperatures, though, only 3,000 fans bothered to watch the first game.

Game 2 moved the series to the Edmonton Arena. The game, with 7,000 fans packed in the stands, did not go as planned—at least as far as the Flyers were concerned. The Senators scored a shocking 3–2 win and evened the series. The Flyers came back to take Game 3 by a 7–0 count, Rollins' fourth shutout of the playoffs. The Flyers won Game 4 with a score of 5–3, and with Game 5 set for Calgary's Victoria Rink, where the hostile fans would be cheering on the Easterners in their quest to deny the Edmontonians their ultimate goal, there was no guarantee that the Flyers would be able to close out the series with ease.

The Stampeders fans performed exactly as expected.

Even though Edmonton was defending the honour of the West against Ottawa, Calgarians filled the Victoria Arena to boo the Flyers and do anything they could to sabotage Edmonton's championship goals. "It boils down to an obvious case of the the vast majority of Calgarians not being big enough to throw season-long jealousies into the ash-can," wrote *Edmonton Journal* columnist Don Fleming.[39] "They're only bushers in the sportsmanship league."

But the Flyers would even the score when it came to national senior amateur championships. The Stampeders skated with the Allan Cup on Edmonton ice in 1946; two years later, with a 5–3 win, the Flyers took the amateur crown on Calgary ice. Clovechok paced the way with a hat trick in the final game, and Rollins finished the team's playoff run with a goals-against average under two. Indeed, he had accomplished in Edmonton what he had set out to do at the start of the season—to keep climbing towards an NHL career.

The Flyers returned to a heroes' welcome the likes of which no Edmonton sports team had seen before. Over 60,000 fans attended a parade in the team's honour. The Flyers had become Edmonton's true hockey heroes—and team captain Gordon Watt was so moved, he decided to name his newborn son Allan in honour of the trophy. Allan Watt would later go on to work for both the Canadian Football League's Edmonton Eskimos and the Oilers.

Glory Days on the Farm

In 1951, the Stamps and the Flyers both agreed to join the pro ranks. Along with the Saskatoon Quakers, the two teams joined the Pacific Coast Hockey League, a minor pro circuit affiliated with the NHL. With the addition of the prairie teams, the PCHL changed its name to the Western Hockey League. The Flyers would become a farm team for the mighty Detroit Red Wings, a powerhouse club that won the Stanley Cup four times from '50–'55. The Stamps linked up with the Chicago Black Hawks, arguably the worst franchise in the league at the time.

It made for an interesting dichotomy. The Flyers were immediately stacked with future Hall of Fame talent. Glenn Hall tended the goal, while (by 1954) local products Norm Ullman and Johnny Bucyk made forays into the opposition zone. Players like Al Arbour and Bronco Horvath added to the toughness of the Flyers. In even a 12-team NHL (which was still a decade and a half from becoming a reality) all of these players would have been stars in the most popular hockey league in the world. However, because the reserve clause allowed the six existing NHL teams to keep players as their property for as long as they wanted, these future superstars waited in the wings for their chances to become Wings.

Meanwhile, the Stampeders team was good enough that it was almost on par with its parent club in Chicago, which regularly floundered at or near the rear of the NHL standings. Parts between the two clubs were interchangeable. It made for a fascinating contrast. "Calgary was as good as Chicago," recalls Hall. "There really was just a fine line between those teams. The problem with Chicago was that they didn't have a farm system until Calgary, and that's when they started building. Detroit had a great farm system. It wasn't until they got Calgary that Chicago started to come up. I think if Calgary would have played Chicago, Chicago would beat them, because they had two or three veterans who might have made a difference. Yes, I think that we (the Edmonton Flyers) would have given them (the NHL Hawks) a game. They probably would have beat us, but we would have made them sweat to do it. For over a hundred years, hockey players have been trying to play this game and avoid sweating; you can't do it. To be successful, you have to give a lot of sweat and bleed a little, too. We would have made Chicago earn it."

Doug Barkley, who played 219 career regular season games with the Stampeders from 1956–62, remembers the great sense of rivalry between the two Alberta WHL teams. "There was always a rivalry with Edmonton, even in junior when I played in Medicine Hat. In fact, it was always a huge event. We always wanted to beat them." Barkley, who enjoyed a solid career with the Red Wings in the '60s until an eye injury forced him to retire in '66 (he later coached the Wings for 88 NHL games during the 1970s), says that Calgary/Edmonton games usually had more than their share of fisticuffs and rough play. "Edmonton/Calgary was always a tough game. They (The Flyers) had some tough battlers, like Howie Young or Pete Goegan. There were a heck of a lot of fights. It was just like it is in the NHL days, even if Calgary misses the playoffs, it was big if they beat Edmonton six out of six or eight out of eight. There were a lot of good players hoping to go up—a lot of good players."

Barkley's sentiments are echoed by former Stamps' teammate Ron "Squeak" Leopold. "It was always Calgary and Edmonton," says Leopold. "It didn't matter at what level you played. The rivalry was there in midget and bantam hockey. I used to play for Calgary Buffalo Athletic Association, which was sponsored by one of the breweries. Each year, we'd play either Edmonton Canadians or Edmonton Maple Leafs in the provincial finals. That's how it was every year. Sometimes we won, sometimes they won. We played those two-game total goal series—and they were intense, I tell you...I remember that when we met in the playoffs the places were really packed. It was a rivalry, all right. Just like Gretzky and the Oilers and the Flames."

"I guess that against Calgary the games were of a higher tempo," says Hall. "But I always enjoyed playing against a good team. And Calgary was a very good team at the time. I felt that they were the top of the Western League. We always played to full houses in Calgary and Edmonton."

Leopold was consistently one of the WHL's top scorers through the '50s and '60s, but never really got a legitimate shot to break into the NHL. In 1960–61, a season before Black Hawk Bobby Hull became the first man in franchise history to score 50 goals in one season, Leopold notched 50 and linemate Lou Jankowski netted 57 for Chicago's farm team. As the Hawks had a Stanley Cup champion team (Chicago had improved dramatically as a franchise since the bottom-of-the-barrel '50s), neither of the Stampeders' stars could get a legitimate shot at leaving the Calgary Corral for the Chicago Stadium.

Hall, who had already made it to the NHL when the Stamps' dynamic duo terrorized the WHL, remembers playing against Jankowski in Ontario junior hockey. "When I was named MVP of the Ontario Hockey League, Lou finished one vote behind me. He was a great junior player; he played with (Alex) Delvecchio in Oshawa. We played together at Indianapolis. But he fractured his skull in his first game of pro. Of course, this was a time before helmets and he was never the same player—he never developed into what he could have been."

Really, there were several different types of players in the WHL:

a) The talented young player who was a good bet to make the NHL, but his parent club felt needed time in the minors to perfect his game;

b) The career minor leaguer who would never get a shot at the NHL;

c) The former NHLer who was sent down in the autumn of his career;

d) The journeyman who continued to bounce up and down from the NHL to the WHL and back again.

Those playing in the modern American Hockey League,

the top farm league of the NHL at the beginning of the 21st century, can make a decent living. But in the days of the Flyers and Stamps, even future NHL stars like Barkley and Hall would only be playing for chump change. For career WHLers like Jankowski and Leopold, what kept them coming back to the WHL year after year wasn't just the hope that one day a scout from the parent club would deem them good enough for promotion (a hope that faded with every passing season), but also a passion for the game.

Leopold says that he simply accepted that time was running out on his NHL dream—but he didn't allow it to curtail his passion for Stampeders' hockey. "At that time it was different; you played junior until you were 20. And if you didn't make it by the time you were 23, you stayed in the minors. There were a lot of good players there. With six teams in the American league, seven or eight in the West and the six NHL teams, there weren't a lot of jobs."

Hall says that the quality of play in the WHL was so good, players felt fortunate to stick with a roster in that league, let alone worry about getting to the NHL. That's something coming from the mouth of a Hall of Famer. "I just used to think how lucky I was to be playing hockey. I didn't have to play in the NHL. I felt that as long as I was playing anywhere, I was happy. I felt that the Western League had a lot of good teams."

"I remember when I first came down from Chicago, and I was told that I was being placed on 24-hour recall, and I felt really good," laughs Barkley. "Then one of the veterans told me that he had spent the last five years on 24-hour recall. That's how it was; teams didn't really care who they sent down...The money was terrible. In my third year of pro

I made $3,500. When I came up to Detroit I was happy because I was making $7,000, which was the minimum."

So even though the Stamps and Flyers were pros, they truly were playing for love of the game—especially the players who knew that their last shots to make the NHL had come and gone. Barkley, like many of his Stamps' teammates, operated a cement mixer during the off-season in order to top up a very modest hockey salary.

But even though both teams harboured dozens of NHL dreams, they were still bitter rivals. That rivalry came to a head in the 1952–53 season. That year's playoffs would mark the first of three consecutive campaigns that the Flyers and the Stamps would battle in the WHL post-season. The Flyers were bolstered by the fact that the Indianapolis Capitols, the Red Wings' other minor league affiliate, folded in the 1952 off-season. So the Flyers became the de facto number one minor league team in the system, and had their lineup bolstered by the top players from the Capitols, including Hall. Despite having Hall, the team struggled during the regular season. The Flyers finished the campaign with a 21–28–11 record (through a quirk in scheduling, the Flyers played 60 games while the rest of the WHL teams played 70). But some of the team's misfortune can be blamed on the fact that Hall spent a portion of the season with the Red Wings, as he was called up to replace the injured Terry Sawchuk.

With the Flyers' fourth-place finish, they would have to play the Stampeders in the first round of the 1953 playoffs. As the Stamps finished the season with a superior 31–27–12 record, they were favoured to take the series rather easily over the Flyers. The Flyers were weakened by the loss of leading scorer Vic Stasiuk, who would later finish in second place in balloting for the WHL's Most Valuable Player award. Stasiuk suffered a dislocated hip after being checked awkwardly into the boards by tough-as-nails Stampeder Gus Kyle in a late, regular season match-up. Flyers playing coach Bud Poile moved himself from his normal spot on the blueline to right wing to fill Stasiuk's slot. Al Arbour, a large defenceman who had impressed in the junior ranks with the Windsor Spitfires (and would later go on to coach the New York Islanders to four straight Stanley Cups from 1980–84), was called up to take Poile's place.

The Stasiuk injury was one of many incidents between the Flyers and Stamps during the final month of the '52–'53 regular season. The Flyers were in the midst of a desperate push to gain a playoff spot. Meanwhile, the Stamps—already assured of a spot in the post-season—did their best to try and prevent Edmonton from reaching that goal. Each and every time the two teams met, it didn't take much to get tempers past the boiling point. The beginning of hostilities can really be traced back to February of 1953. Stampeder Steve Witiuk fractured the jaw of Flyer Jack MacDonald in a game at the Calgary Corral. The incident set off a series of fights between the teams in a two-game back-to-back weekend series. Poile was disciplined by WHL president Al Leader after he promised the local sportswriter that blood would spill in the Edmonton Gardens rematch. "Besides, Coach Poile was hauled up on the carpet by League President Al Leader for a radio broadcast on the afternoon of the game wherein he suggested that fans would do well to see the game because there would be lots popping."[40]

The playoffs would provide yet another turn in the

rivalry. Instead of a rout by the Stampeders, what fans got was the kind of edge-of-your-seat entertainment that the Flames and Oilers would provide three decades later. These were indeed the best of times for postwar Alberta. Premier Ernest Manning had just announced that the province would spend $174 million in its new budget, which set an Alberta spending record. The oil boom was in full swing; the province declared revenues of over $40 million in 1953, a $7 million increase over 1952. The playoff series would be more than a battle between hockey clubs; it would be a sporting spectacle between two cities that were looking boldly towards a bright future.

The best-of-five series opened at the Corral, but the sold-out crowd was silenced when the Flyers snatched a 3–0 lead, powered by two goals from Ching Johnson. The Stamps battled back to make it 3–2, but they could not get a tying marker past Hall. After the game, Poile, who enjoyed using the media to psych out the opposition and rally his players, sent a message to Stampeders' fans and coach Hank Blade through his favourite reporter, the *Edmonton Journal*'s Don Fleming. "My heart bleeds for them, but the fans down here (Calgary) will be seeing their last game of hockey when we take on the Stampeders again. The series won't come back to Calgary, and Blade and his guys will have cashed in their chips by next Monday."[41]

Poile's bluster certainly inspired Flyers forward Earl Reibel; with just 39 seconds left in Game 2 of the series, he rifled the winning goal past Stamps goalie Phil Hughes. The Flyers eked out a 5–4 win and were looking to sweep the series at home—and make their coach look like a hockey Nostradamus. Instead of capitulating, the Stampeders fought on—and engineered one of the greatest comebacks in the history of Alberta playoff hockey. A record crowd of 7,575 fans packed the Edmonton Gardens for Game 3 and went home disappointed. The Stamps triumphed by a 4–2 count, but the score alone did not tell the whole story. The Stamps fired 44 shots at Hall, and the future Vezina Trophy winner was the man who stopped his team from being blown out of their own rink.

Kyle also renewed his role in the Alberta rivalry, as he became the centre of a major brouhaha between the two clubs and the Edmonton police. Kyle had hit Flyer Larry Wilson, who had been playing on a bad knee, and Kyle's hit took the Flyers' forward out of the series. Later in the game, Kyle and Flyer Larry Zeidel got into a tussle and both players raised their sticks. They were sent to the penalty box, where a lone police officer was the only thing that separated the two. That officer could not stop hostilities between Zeidel and Kyle from escalating in the box. It took several police officers, who had come to the sin bin from other points in the arena, to break up the pair. "Kyle had his sweater badly torn and he had to make a change, but the big loser was a policeman who decided to sit between the pair in the hoosegow."[42]

Calgary ended up sweeping the two games in Edmonton, and returned home to the Corral sure that they had the momentum needed to finish their comeback. At 6:48 of the third period, they could have been forgiven for beginning their celebrations prematurely. After all, the Stamps had just taken a 5–2 lead—and were greatly outplaying the Flyers, who were using just four defenceman and eight forwards because of their injury problems. Not only was Stasiuk on the shelf, but Reibel, who had scored the winner in Game 2, was out because of chronic knee pain. Wilson, who had earlier been declared out for the remainder of the series, played on his bad knee. But goals by Len Haley and Jim Anderson brought the Flyers back to 5–4—and then came the miracle. Ray Hannigan, a journeyman who had played three games in the NHL with the Toronto Maple Leafs, beat Hughes with just eight seconds left in regulation to send the game into overtime.

The Stamps, of course, were stunned. Their surprise turned to horror when Hannigan struck again in overtime. The beaten-up Flyers squad had somehow found a way to make up a three-goal third-period deficit and win the series. While Hannigan got the headlines the next day, Hall's role in the game could not be ignored. The Stamps outshot the Flyers by a 45–20 margin, but ended up losing the game because Hall outduelled Hughes.

Of course, fortune might have something to do with the win, too. "I remember we had such a great series with Calgary," says Hall. "It was famous that the road team won each and every game. And I remember in the fifth game we were down 5–2 and we came back to win in overtime. We got the breaks. And don't think that a few breaks aren't that important. It's so important to be lucky in hockey, and we were that night." The Flyers would go on to win the 1953 WHL championship, but it was the series with the Stampeders that presented their greatest obstacle to the President's Trophy.

During the season that the Flyers won their first WHL championship, they became linked with their Calgary rivals. During the 1952–53 season, Chicago Black Hawks' owner Bill Tobin sold his interest in the team to the Norris family and Arthur Wirtz. The deal, which would be forbidden under modern NHL rules that prevent a company or person from controlling more than one team at the same time, stunk to high heaven. The Norrises already controlled the Detroit Red Wings, and Wirtz had divested himself of his Wings shares to make the Chicago deal. As the Wings were at the height of their dynasty at the time of the purchase, it was made clear to the NHL and all the players on the two teams that the Black Hawks would be treated as a de facto farm team of the Wings. By the mid-1950s, the Norris and Wirtz empires had separated their businesses. The Norrises took over full control of the Red Wings while Wirtz got the Hawks. But neither camp shook suspicions of collusion.

When the deal was made, Hall says players on the Stamps and Flyers realized that they had become part of one loosely connected organization. "Because of the family ties, there was a lot of player movement between the two teams. Management wanted to put the good players in Detroit and the bad players in Chicago. Or they also sent the players that didn't toe the line to Chicago." Detroit players were constantly threatened by trades to last-place Chicago if they did not toe the line in the Motor City. In 1957, those threats were carried out when Hall—who by then had already established himself as an elite NHLer—and fellow future Hall of Famer Ted Lindsay were dispatched to the Hawks. Why? Widespread league concern that the two were plotting to launch a players' union. Ironically, Hall led the Hawks to a '61 Cup win over the Red Wings. The inmates of the distant gulag had beaten their Detroit masters.

Even though the players were aware of what was basically a merger of the Wings and the Hawks, they didn't let
it affect the way they approached the games down on the
farm in the Western Hockey League. "I would say that it
never crossed my mind," says Leopold. "You signed your
C-form and you didn't think too much else other than who
you played for. You were either Chicago or Detroit. I was
Chicago." (A C-form was the basic entry contract for a player signing with an NHL team. It allowed the team to place
the player with any team the organization saw fit, and also
forbade the player from negotiating with any other NHL
club.)

The spring of 1954 ushered in a new era in the hockey
world. As the Stamps and Flyers got set to meet in the second round of the playoffs, the Dynamo Moscow team beat
Canada in the final game of the World Championships, beginning a new Soviet dynasty in the international game.

The Stamps began the 1953–54 season with a 9–0
drubbing of the Flyers. It sent a message to Edmonton
that their provincial rivals would not show the defending
league champs any respect. But their playoff series would
be markedly closer than that first game. Even though the
Flyers barely scraped into the playoffs while the Stamps
finished atop the WHL standings, the two teams sported
9–9–1 records against each other during the season. In
1954, the WHL extended the playoff series from best-of-five
to best-of-seven, and the two teams would be taking each
other to the limit.

Having finished first in the WHL standings, Calgary secured home ice advantage for the duration of the playoffs.
They hosted the Flyers in Game 1, and 7,995 packed the

Corral to see the home team take an early 2–0 lead only to blow it. Frank Currie, who had coached the Flyers in their days as a senior amateur squad, was the new coach of the Stampeders—and he had to wring his hands as his charges were forced to overtime by the Flyers. Of course, the memories of last year's overtime loss on Corral ice to the Flyers was still fresh in the minds of both Stamps' players and fans, so when Calgary's George Pargeter beat Hall nearly three minutes into the extra frame, there was a feeling throughout Cowtown that the team had shaken the Edmonton bugaboo.

But, according to Calgary hockey pundit Gorde Hunter, the game would not have gone to overtime if it wasn't for the goaltending of Hall. His report claimed that Calgary had actually outplayed the Eskimos well enough to win by a few goals. "Must say something must be done about this fellow Glen (sic) Hall. Never saw anyone get away with so much out and out robbery in front of so many people. Not taking away anything from the rest of the Flyers, who played very well indeed, Hall was the dominating factor for three full periods. He made miraculous saves and made them look fairly easy." [43]

But the game would not finish without incident. The Stamps claimed that forward Archie Scott received a leg injury when he was kneed by Flyers defender Hugh Coflin. Flyers' captain Jimmy Uniac said he was the victim of a spear during the game, delivered by none other than his team's Public Enemy Number One, Gus Kyle.

A veteran of 203 NHL games with the New York Rangers and Boston Bruins, Kyle was a tough, stay-at-home defenceman, but he wasn't dirty by any means. In only one of the three full seasons he spent as a Stamp (he retired just seven games into the '55–'56 season and took over as the Stamps' head coach in 1957) did Kyle break the 100-penalty-minute barrier.

Game 2 was not as close. The Stamps pounded the Flyers by a 7–1 count. The hero of the day was Pat Lundy, who was coming off his best-ever WHL season, averaging over a point per game. Lundy got two goals and two assists against the Flyers that night. Before coming to the Stamps, Lundy had spent 150 games with the Red Wings and the Black Hawks. Lundy was a gentleman on the ice; not only could he score key goals, he rarely saw the penalty box. Throughout his pro career, the most penalty minutes the Saskatoon native was ever assessed in a season was a measly 21.

Heading back to Edmonton, the Flyers faced a must-win situation. The fact the team was down two games to none did not deter the Edmonton fans; over 7,300 showed up at the Arena for Game 3. They would not go home disappointed. Thanks to Hall's outstanding play in goal and two goals from player/coach Poile and one from his brother Don, the Flyers triumphed 5–2. The Flyers repeated the 5–2 score in Game 4. It was a comfortable win marked by just one fight, as Hannigan dropped the gloves with—whom else—Kyle. The Stamps and Flyers split Games 5 and 6—each team held home ice with two-goal wins. Hall was the star of both games. In Game 5, he held the Flyers into a game in which they were outplayed well into the third period. It wasn't until late in the third that Jim McFadden, who had been dispatched to the WHL that year after spending nearly a decade with the Red Wings and the Black Hawks, showed his veteran savvy and got the game-winner.

"'The Flyers shouldn't even be in the same league as the Stampeders,' an Edmonton sports writer, who obviously must remain anonymous, stated Wednesday night at the Corral. 'But then there's Hall.'" wrote Hunter in the sports pages of the *Calgary Herald*, repudiating the more conciliatory tone of his hockey column just a week earlier.[44]

So, for the second time in as many years, a Flyers/ Stamps playoff series would come down to a single game at the Calgary Corral. A record crowd of 8,900 jammed the arena, breaking the record of 8,538 set when the Stamps (then an amateur senior team) played the Flyers on the Corral's first night of hockey, December 26, 1950.

Calgary, despite the heartbreaking loss to the Flyers the previous playoffs, had enjoyed great support that season. In 1953–54, the Stamps drew 191,822 fans, setting a WHL attendance record. The home fans got nothing close to a repeat of the previous season. Paced by hat tricks from both Lundy and teammate Sid Finney—who had been up and down between the Hawks and Stamps that season—the Stamps blasted Edmonton by an 8–0 count. If there was a game that Hall could display as proof of his assessment that the Stamps were as good as the NHL Hawks, this would have been it. He was shelled all night long by the Calgary shooters, who—knowing what had happened the season before—were determined to make sure that Edmonton had no chance of coming back.

The win came as a relief for Calgary hockey fans, who had last tasted a major victory with the Allan Cup title in 1946. Since then, they had got used to being cannon fodder for the Edmonton hockey club. Not only did the Stamps avenge the 1953 upset, they also gave a major boost to the psyches of battered Calgary sports fans. "Prior to Monday night, the Edmonton situation was getting downright embarrassing and touchy," wrote Hunter. "These northerners, and quite a few Calgarians, too, had reached the conclusion that Calgary would never beat Edmonton in any major sport."[45] Just as the Flyers had used their win over the Stamps to launch a championship run in '53, Calgary used the win over Edmonton as a stepping stone to a WHL title. The Stamps went on to dispose of the Vancouver Canucks in the President's Cup final.

Lagging Spirits: The Duke of Edinburgh Cup

In 1954, a new series was created that would pit the winner of the WHL against the champions from the East. The Duke of Edinburgh Cup series would determine which was the world's best pro hockey team outside of the National Hockey League. The Stamps met the AHL champ Quebec Aces in the final. The Stamps won the best-of-nine final in just six games. But the Duke of Edinburgh Cup did not capture the imagination of Calgarians like their Stamps' playoff battles with the Flyers. While a decent crowd of over 6,500 watched the Stamps win the D of E Cup, attendance for the series was well short of the standing-room-only crowds that flocked to the Corral when the Flyers were in town. In the hearts and minds of Calgarians, beating Edmonton was more important than winning a championship.

In 1955, the Flyers were bolstered by the addition of two players who had been standouts for the junior hockey powerhouse Edmonton Oil Kings—Johnny Bucyk and Norm Ullman. Both would go onto Hall of Fame careers in

the National Hockey League, and the 1954–55 WHL season was their jumping-off point to greatness. That year,
Bronco Horvath led the WHL in scoring with 110 points in
just 67 games played; Bucyk finished with 88 in 70, while
Ullman got 67 even though he missed a significant chunk
of time to injury. The Flyers, used to scrapping for a playoff spot late into the season, were the cream of the league
in 1955. With a 39–20–11 record, the Flyers finished 15
points ahead of the Victoria Cougars atop the WHL standings. Meanwhile, the Stamps went through the season not
looking like anything close to defending Duke of Edinburgh
Cup champions; they stumbled into the post-season with
a .500 record.

The Flyers' rise as a power coincided with a new op-
timism in the Alberta capital. According to a city study
commissioned right before the start of the WHL playoffs,
Edmonton was forecast to have a population of 400,000 by
1980! (Actually, the city beat those projections handily.)

Just as in 1953 and 1954, the Stamps and Flyers would
meet in the playoffs. This time, it would be Edmonton who
held home ice advantage and would go into the series as
favourites. Unlike the previous two series, the 1955 all-
Alberta playoff encounter would not be taken to the limit; in fact, it wasn't even close. The Stamps' hopes would
soon be up in flames. A 4–2 win by the Flyers in Game 1,
sparked by a two-goal effort from Lorne Davis, set the stage
for a clean sweep. The Flyers would go on to their second
WHL championship in three years, and they would earn
the right to claim the Duke of Edinburgh Cup just as their
southern rivals had done the year before.

The Flyers were set to play Shawinigan Falls in the best-of-nine series, held in different venues throughout Quebec. Even though the Stamps had been eliminated by the Flyers, their spectre still haunted their Edmonton rivals. Quebec officials had been stung in 1954 when their beloved Quebec Aces had been trounced by Calgary. So, they made sure that the Quebec champs would have every advantage possible in the 1955 championship.

George Gravel, a referee who had been hand-picked by Quebec hockey officials, became the bane of the Flyers. After losing the first two games, coach Poile requested that Gravel be removed. In Game 1, Gravel assessed 14 of 18 penalties to Edmonton, and 25 of 40 penalty calls to the Flyers in Game 2. Those two games would be the springboard to Shawinigan Falls' upset series win over the Flyers. "It was prearranged," is all that Hall of Fame goalie Glenn Hall will say about that series.

As the teams played in the late '50s, having a TV was still a special thing. For most Albertans, there was no danger of *Hockey Night in Canada* keeping them away from either the Edmonton Gardens or the Calgary Corral on a Saturday night. Yes, Alberta fans followed the NHL as best as they could, but when it came to taking the family out or a night out with the boys, hockey—along with the football Eskimos and Stampeders—was the thing to do.

As the '60s arrived, the popularity of the WHL began to wane in Alberta. As TVs continued to penetrate into Alberta houses and more and more hockey fans decided to stay home and watch the NHL on *Hockey Night in Canada* rather than go to the rink, minor pro hockey in Western Canada began to lose steam.

Former Flyer ('55–'59) Frank Roggeveen believes that

the Flyers/Stamps rivalry of the late '50s was not as fierce as the rivalry the two franchises had when they were still amateur teams before 1951. "I really didn't feel that there was that much special between ourselves and Calgary. I remember that we wanted to beat anyone in the league who we played. The rivalry really started to dwindle, and the crowds started to dwindle, in the late '50s. There was hockey on TV then, and the people had more choices on what they could do. There were football games to go to. They didn't have that back in the senior days; the Flyers were the only show in town. And the old senior league only had four teams: Calgary, Edmonton, Regina and Saskatoon. There was Lethbridge too, for a little while, but the league was so small that Calgary and Edmonton had to have a great rivalry."

Still, ex-Stampeder Doug Barkley recalls many nights when the Corral was absolutely jammed with people there to see the Stamps play. "When the Flames played there in the '80s, you got 8,000 or 9,000 in the Corral. Back then, it was full with 6,000 or 7,000 fans. And it was full all the time." And when the two teams played, the game was far more interactive than it is now. "There was no glass on the sides at the time," recalls Barkley. "So you would go right into the crowd. So, if you were hit, you were pushed into the crowd—and the crowd would push you right back...The Edmonton and Calgary fans—they probably disliked each other more than the players did."

But even though the fans would get the chance to shove the players if they got too close for comfort, Hall recalls that, in true Canadian fashion, there was always a pervading sense of politeness in both the Gardens and the Corral.

Calgary Fire Brigade Hockey Team, 1894–95. (Glenbow Archives, NA-2854-129)

Edmonton's Thistle Hockey Club, Alberta champions 1903. (Provincial Archives of Alberta, B6542)

Edmonton's Thistle hockey rink, 1900. (Provincial Archives of Alberta, B6528)

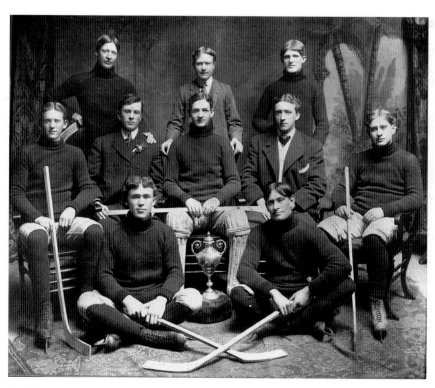

The Calgary Hockey Club, ca. 1904–05. (Glenbow Archives, NA-1280-4)

Hockey game at Edmonton arena, 1921—note the goal judge standing behind the net.
(Glenbow Archives, NC-6-6323)

Interior of arena, exhibition grounds, Calgary. (Glenbow Archives NA-3965-49)

Goaltender Toban of the Edmonton Eskimos, 1921. (Glenbow Archives NC-6-7062)

Edmonton Eskimos, 1925-26. *Back row*: Goldsworthy, Stanley, Keats, McKenzie (manager), Shore, Benson, and McIntyre. *Front row*: Boucher, Sparrow, Stuart, Gagne, Anderson, and Sheppard.
(Glenbow Archives, ND-3-3136)

Left to right: Eskimos Shore, Gagne, Stuart, and Keats, 1926. (Glenbow Archives, ND-3-3112b)

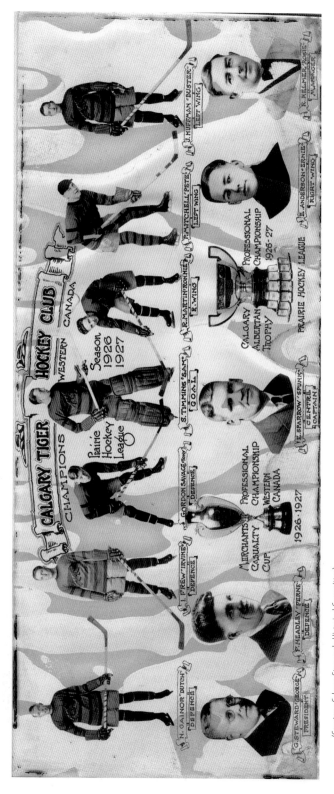

(Courtesy, Calgary Stampede Historical Committee)

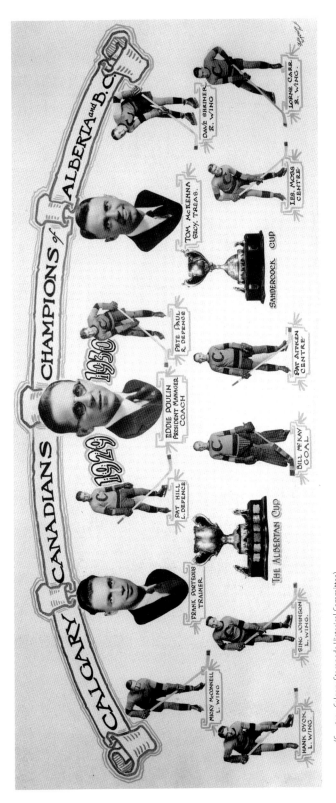

(Courtesy, Calgary Stampede Historical Committee)

(Provincial Archives of Alberta, A12905)

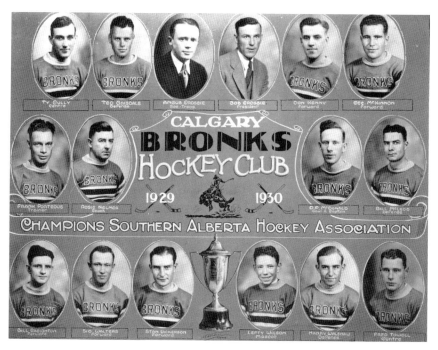

(Courtesy, Calgary Stampede Historical Committee)

Above: Dave "Sweeney" Schriner hams it up for the camera. (City of Edmonton Archives EA-600-847D)

Left: Referee Clarence Campbell in pre-whistle days, 1929—note the bell in his left hand. (Provincial Archives of Alberta, A12897)

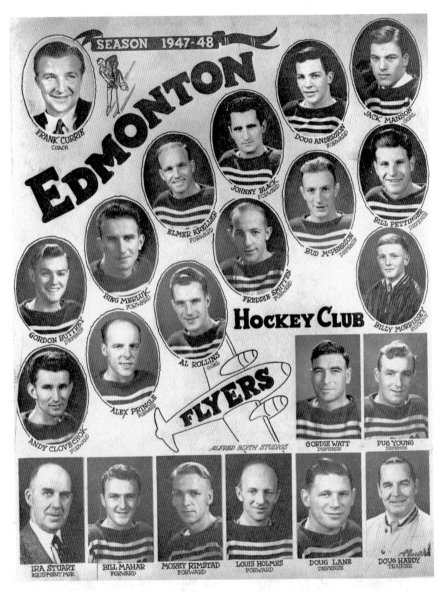

(Provincial Archives of Alberta, BL2721)

Calgary Stampeders Allan Cup champions, 1946. (Courtesy, Calgary Stampede Historical Committee)

Edmonton stars of a half-century ago.

Edmonton Flyers goaltender Glenn Hall stands up to a Stampeder charge, 1954.
(Glenbow Archives NA-5600-7807f)

Left to right: Calgary Stampeders Couture, Finney, and Scott, 1956-57.
(Courtesy, Calgary Stampede Historical Committee)

(Courtesy, Calgary Stampede Historical Committee)

Left to right: Calgary Stampeders Dzurko, Houghton, Fogolin, Michaluk, and Barkley, 1956-57.
(Courtesy, Calgary Stampede Historical Committee)

The Oilers' Lee Fogolin shakes up a Flame. (*The Edmonton Journal*)

opposite page top: Neil Sheehy of the Flames.
(Courtesy of the Calgary Flames Hockey Club)
opposite page bottom: Dave Semenko of the Oilers.
(*The Edmonton Journal*)

Tim Hunter of the Flames. (Courtesy of the Calgary Flames Hockey Club)

While the two sets of fans truly didn't like each other, it's not as if the atmosphere got overly abusive. "Calgary and Edmonton fans were traditional Canadian hockey fans— they weren't very vocal, but they were very supportive," says Hall. "When we played in Calgary, the place wasn't very loud, but we sure knew who they were cheering for. The same was true in Edmonton. It wasn't really until that most recent Stanley Cup (in 2004) when Canadian fans started yelling and screaming."

While former Stamps star Jankowski says that going to Edmonton Gardens was the toughest part of the Stampeders schedule, no matter how good or bad the Flyers, he agrees that while the players relished the rivalry, they never felt any ill will from the fans beyond the usual acrimony shown to the visiting team. "It was always tougher to play in the Edmonton Gardens. They played just that much better at home. But the fans were never a problem...they always had real good fans."

Ron "Squeak" Leopold says that neither the Edmonton Gardens nor the Stampede Corral had glass over the boards. Both arenas still used chicken wire long after the six NHL clubs had made glass standard in their rinks. "You had the boards on the sides and that was it. At each end there were wire fences. And on a lot of nights you ended up with your face pushed into the fence."

But as much as the two teams battled on the ice, there was a code of honour between the players. There was a lot of respect, too. Barkley recalls a real rough game from the '61–'62 season when he and Flyers' tough-guy Howie Young squared off a couple of times. Later in the game, Young was prone on the ice and couldn't defend himself from an oncoming shot. Barkley got in the way. "We had two fights in the game but I still protected him," says Barkley matter-of-factly. That was simply the way things were done.

Barkley also remembers playing alongside Flyers' star Jim "Bud" MacPherson in a WHL All-Star Game held at the Edmonton Gardens. When they were together in the dressing room, Barkley even managed to crack a joke with his old enemy. "When he had his pads off I saw he was as big as a blacksmith. He was built like a tree. I said to him, 'I'm real worried about challenging you again.'"

Young was a key part of the Flyers '62 championship run. Sent down to the farm by the Red Wings earlier in the '61–'62 season, Young was so despised by the Calgary fans that the Herald even took out space in its sports section to encourage fans to boo the Flyers' tough guy. "Number one Edmonton Flyer menace and an absolute fiend as far as most Calgary Stampeder hockey fans are concerned," wrote the *Herald* as the Flyers faced their rivals in the '62 Northern final.[46]

In 1962, the Flyers were the toast of the Northern Division. By finishing at the top of the standings, they earned a bye into the finals, with their opponent being decided out of a preliminary best-of-three series between the Stampeders and the Seattle Totems. The Stamps won handily, setting up the last hurrah of their famous rivalry. The two would square off in the Northern final.

The Stamps travelled to Edmonton immediately after beating the Totems 5–3 in the clinching game of their series at the Corral. The Stamps were a much different team than the powerhouse of the mid-'50s. They were no longer interchangeable with the parent club in Chicago, as Hall suggested they were back in the early days of the WHL. The Black Hawks were now one of the NHL elite; not only did they feature Hall as arguably the best goaltender in the NHL at that time, but also future Hall of Famers Stan Mikita and Bobby Hull, as well as Norris Trophy-winning defenceman Pierre Pilote. They were the '61 Stanley Cup champs, and in '62 would make it to the final again, only to be vanquished by the Toronto Maple Leafs. These Stamps did not wait on pins and needles every day for the call to come from the Windy City. This was a team filled with players who knew that they were likely to play in the WHL for a long time.

The Stamps skated on Edmonton Gardens ice for Game 1 of the series less than 24 hours after eliminating Seattle, while the Flyers team waited nine days for the series. The Stamps' fatigue showed for most of the game. The Flyers held a 4–2 lead with 1:12 left in regulation, but the Stamps rallied with two late goals to send the game into overtime. Before Game 1, the Stamps had not lost an OT battle throughout the '61–'62 season. But that would come to an end in the first overtime frame when Flyer veteran Billy McNeill, who had been up and down between Edmonton and Detroit over the past decade, banged in the winner.

The Game 1 attendance number, just over 4,300, showed how much the Flyers had slipped in the eyes of the Edmonton sports fan since the glory days of the '50s, when the Edmonton Gardens were jammed with over 7,000 fans for a playoff game against the hated Stamps.

According to the *Calgary Herald*'s match report, Game 1 was by no means a clean affair—referee Lloyd Gilmour had a rough time trying to break up several stick fights. "They were hitting with everything but the proverbial kitchen sink," wrote George Bilych. "And they weren't sparing the sticks any. The hickory was coming up every time the combatants came into close quarters and even though Lloyd Gilmour called a spearing and several high-sticking calls, he missed at least as many."[47]

"I just remember that the games were always part of a real tough rivalry," recalls Jankowski, who was on the Stamps' first line for that '62 playoff series. "They were real tough games to play...not really a lot of fighting, but a lot of hitting."

After catching their breath, the Stampeders came out roaring in Game 2. Ed Babiuk—an Edmonton native who would only play the '61–'62 season with the Stamps—was stellar in the Stamps net, and Leopold provided two goals to propel the Calgarians to a 4–2 win over the rivals and spark talk of an upset. Those hopes were displayed by the 7,487 fans who came to the Corral to see Game 3. The series, despite Edmonton being the favourite, was generating far more fan interest in the south.

But the Flyers spoiled the party. Backstopped by the solid play of netminder Gilles Boisvert, who made it to the Red Wings for all of three NHL appearances, and thanks to key goals from Eddie Joyal and Doug Messier (Mark's father), the Flyers went on to a 4–2 win, which Poile guaranteed would pop the balloon of hope that the Stampeders' players and fans had inflated. "There's only one man on the entire Stampeder club that has us a trifle concerned," boasted Poile before Game 4. "The only thing that's kept them in so far has been Ed Babiuk. He's been giving them fantastic goaltending. But I figure we'll get to him, too."[48] Poile's words were prophetic. Not only did the Flyers—

thanks to two-goal performances from Len Lunde and Roger DeJordy—go on to a convincing 5–2 win, only 4,736 paid to see it at the Corral. Calgarians had deserted the Stamps after their Game 3 loss.

Over 5,500 fans—still less than a full house—came to the Edmonton Gardens to see Messier score twice and the Flyers win Game 5 by a 9–2 score. Despite Poile's claims that his '62 Flyers were every bit as good as, and maybe better than, the Flyers' glory teams of '53 and '55, these Flyers were not celebrities in Edmonton as were their championship predecessors. Even though the Flyers were stomped in the first two games of the WHL final by the Spokane Comets, they rallied to take the series in seven games. Only 4,800 fans came out to see the Flyers' Game 7 win.

The Flyers and Stamps would battle growing fan disinterest for another season. In the summer of '63, both teams left Alberta behind, and the WHL league stayed south of the 49th parallel. All that was left were memories of the fierce hockey rivalry the two teams had pursued since the game was first played on frozen ponds and rivers in the province.

If the Flyers and Stampeders had such a great rivalry, one that lasted for the better part of two decades, why is it not better remembered by the fans in either Calgary or Edmonton? Why are there no banners commemorating the Flyers' WHL championships hanging next to the Oilers' Stanley Cup banners at Rexall Place, or even at the Northlands Agricom, which sits on the same parcel of land where the Edmonton Gardens once stood? Why aren't there more teary remembrances of the great Stampeders past on Calgary sports radio or newspapers? Why are the memories of the Stamps limited to fading photos that adorn the walls of the old Corral?

We have become dependent on visual media for our sports fix. To remember the great moments in sports history, we need to see the video proof. When we talk about Bobby Thompson's shot heard round the world, it's not enough for us to know the story of the Giants nipping the Dodgers for the National League pennant. We need to see the grainy black-and-white footage of Thompson leaping around the basepaths like a child on Christmas morning. We need to see Bobby Orr flying through the air, arms held high in celebration after scoring the Cup-winning goal. We need to see Michael Jordan leaping towards the basket. Any great sporting event that doesn't have the accompanying video is now lost to us. We don't recall the great Ottawa Senators teams of the '20s, and while there is a pitching award named for the great Cy Young, we'd all be hard pressed to recall for which team he played.

There were no cameras recording those games at the Corral and the Gardens. The lore of the Flyers and Stampeders can only be found in old newspaper articles and through the stories from the teams' alumni. "You look back on it, and you see that the new generation has video and that sort of stuff, and they can see all the great players," says Leopold. "They didn't have that when we played. I remember that they (Edmonton) had so many great players...and they go on in the people's memories who were at the arenas, and the stories that they tell and the old newspapers and magazines." But Jankowski, Barkley and Leopold still try and keep that team spirit alive. They still meet regularly for coffee and to chat about what's happen-

ing in the world of hockey. Every once in a while, they remember those heady days when Stamps' hockey fuelled the
passion of Calgary sports fans during those long Alberta
winters.

Cowboys and Oil: The Rivalry That Never Happened

Ever since hockey was first played in Alberta, Calgary and Edmonton were rivals. When one city got to a provincial or championship, the city that wasn't competing would jealously cheer for the opposition. But Bill Hunter, the innovative Saskatchewan-bred businessman who had managed the junior powerhouse Edmonton Oil Kings and helped found the junior Western Hockey League, had a different vision.

Hunter was recruited by American businessmen Gary Davidson and Dennis Murphy, founders of the American Basketball Association, a rival league of the National Basketball Association. Murphy and Davidson planned to do to the NHL what they had done to the NBA: create a rival league that would change the face of the sport. In 1971, the duo incorporated the World Hockey Association, and Hunter was placed in charge of rallying businessmen to place franchises from coast to coast.

Hunter was a natural huckster. A fiery competitor, Hunter had asked then Prime Minister Pierre Trudeau to invoke the War Measures Act when it looked like the Quebec Remparts might refuse to host the Oil Kings for the 1971 Memorial Cup. The FLQ crisis had made the Quebec hosts edgy; they eventually agreed to the final without interference from Ottawa. The Remparts, led by Guy Lafleur, throttled Hunter's Oil Kings in the final.

The WHA was scheduled to begin play in the autumn of 1972, so Hunter had a year to get potential owners. A key part of his plan was to have teams in both Edmonton and Calgary. He was successful in hooking up with broadcasting mogul Dr. Charles Allard and businessman Zane Feldman to back a franchise, to be called the Edmonton Oilers, which would play out of the Gardens. An expansion franchise was awarded to a group based out of Calgary, to be called the Broncos, reminiscent of the amateur hockey powerhouse of the 1930s. When it came time for the franchise owners to pony up the fees needed to be included in the new league, however, neither Calgary nor the Miami Screaming Eagles were able to come up with the funds.

Devastated by the loss of a rival Calgary franchise, Hunter had a novel idea, one that would attempt to bridge the hockey gap between the two Alberta cities. He wanted the Oilers franchise that had been awarded to his consortium to split its home games between the Edmonton Gardens and the Calgary Stampede Corral. Instead of being known as the "Edmonton" Oilers, the team would be known as the "Alberta" Oilers.

The team carried the Alberta Oilers name when it faced off in the WHA opener against the Ottawa Nationals on October 11, 1972, even though no deal was in place for any home games at the Corral. That deal would never happen.

The Oilers would miss the playoffs in their inaugural season, but the team was buoyed by news that a new arena, one that would rival anything in the NHL, would be built on the Northlands fairgrounds just a stone's throw from the Gardens.

By the fall of 1973, the team had changed its name to the "Edmonton" Oilers, signifying that the plan to split any of the business with Calgary had been abandoned. A year later, 15,326 fans came to the new Northlands Coliseum to see the Oilers, led by future Hall of Famer Jacques Plante, beat the Cleveland Crusaders, led by goaltending legend Gerry Cheevers, in the team's home opener.

While the Oilers were a stable member of the WHA, the league itself was on precarious ground. By the mid-'70s, rumours abounded that the powerful Houston Aeros franchise, which featured Gordie Howe and his sons in the line-up, were secretly negotiating with the NHL in hopes of defecting from the WHA. So when businessman Jim Pattison decided to move the Vancouver Blazers to the Calgary Corral to begin play as the Calgary Cowboys in the 1975–76 World Hockey Association season, there were more than a few skeptics who thought he was nuts. After all, the Corral held just 7,000 fans. How could a team that was bleeding money in Vancouver hope to recover in a small arena where the top ticket cost just $9, in a league that was unstable as a Third World government?

While Edmonton/Calgary games had captured the attention of fans in both cities since 1895, the reaction was lukewarm to a new World Hockey Association rivalry. On November 11, 1975, the two teams met for the first time in regular season action. Danny Lawson, Calgary's lead-

ing scorer at the time, had a goal and two assists in the
Cowboys' 6–3 win. The attendance at the Corral was just
4,109; there were plenty of empty seats in the Corral that
night. In the 1950s, Calgary Stampeders WHL home games
against the Edmonton Flyers would often get overflow
crowds of more than 8,000. Even though the population
bases of the two cities had skyrocketed by the mid-'70s,
and the WHA was trying to sell itself as a major league that
could rival the NHL, a Cowboys/Oilers game struggled to
get half that number.

Empty seats were in evidence when the two teams
played again November 30 at Northlands Coliseum. Just
8,885 fans—about half of what Northlands Coliseum could
hold—went to see coach Clare Drake's Oilers get their revenge with a 4–2 win, with defenceman Skip Krake getting
both the winning goal and insurance marker.

While a Cowboys/Oilers rivalry never materialized, the
Calgarians were one of the great surprises in the WHA.
In '75–'76, the Cowboys finished six games over the .500
mark, thanks to a 44-goal season from Lawson and 42
more from future Oilers' captain Ron Chipperfield. Once
the Cowboys got to the playoffs, they became embroiled
in one of the ugliest incidents in pro hockey history.
They opened their first-ever WHA post-season with a series against the Quebec Nordiques, one of the Cadillac
franchises of the league. At Quebec City's Le Colisée,
Cowboy and native Edmontonian Rick Jodzio came off
the bench and attacked Marc Tardif with his stick, beating the Nordiques star and WHA scoring leader so badly
that Tardif was left with brain injuries. It was the kind of
premeditated attack that typified the kind of slug-it-out

brawlfest hockey that was typical of the movie *Slap Shot*. The story will no doubt remind today's hockey fans of Vancouver Canuck Todd Bertuzzi's attack on Steve Moore of the Colorado Avalanche near the end of the 2003–04 NHL regular season. Moore ended up with a severe concussion and broken neck vertebrae. The NHL elected to suspend Bertuzzi indefinitely (the suspension was lifted before the start of the 2005–06 season).

The Jodzio attack occurred in the height of hockey's most violent period. The mid-'70s were ruled by the NHL's Philadelphia Flyers, a team that set records for brawls and penalty minutes. The Flyers won Stanley Cups in 1974 and 1975, so commentators and coaches in both the WHA and NHL decided that bloody acts of violence were the acts of champions. That acceptance of violence is one of the reasons why Jodzio's attack will never be remembered the same way Bertuzzi's actions will.

The Cowboys ended up upsetting the Nordiques in the first round, but were eliminated by Bobby Hull and the powerhouse Winnipeg Jets in the next series. Fan interest never picked up, even though the Cowboys made the playoffs. Pattison was bleeding money as less than 5,000 fans per game showed up to see their home team take on the Jets. A year later, Cowboys attendance plummeted to less than 4,500 per game. When a season ticket drive designed to stimulate advance sales for the 1977–78 season stalled, the Cowboys franchise folded.

While the Cowboys died, the Oilers survived. Even though the WHA was doomed, rumours persisted that some WHA teams would survive as NHL expansion clubs. The Oilers boasted a solid fan base, and while the team was not a powerhouse like the Aeros, New England Whalers, Nordiques or Jets, they were a solid bet to survive if the NHL did offer the WHA teams a series of lifelines.

But the Oilers made their most significant move early in the 1978–79 season, which would turn out to be the WHA's final campaign. Teenage sensation Wayne Gretzky, who the Indianapolis Racers had signed as an underage free agent right out of the junior Sault Ste. Marie Greyhounds, was put up for sale just a month into the season. Oilers owner Peter Pocklington jumped at the chance to get the hockey world's most-talked-about teenager into the fold, all for the price of $850,000. The Oilers also got forward Peter Driscoll and goaltender Eddie Mio in the deal, but Gretzky was obviously the focal point of Pocklington's attention. Gretzky was a smash hit in Edmonton. He would score 43 goals and add 61 assists in 72 games as an Oiler, and help the team to its first-ever first place finish in the WHA.

As the Oilers wrapped up the regular season title in the spring of '79, the WHA and NHL announced that they had come to a tentative deal on a merger. The Oilers, Jets, Whalers and Nordiques would survive as new members of the NHL (the Aeros folded the year before), while the rest of the WHA would disappear at the end of the 1978–79 season. But Edmonton fans were dismayed when the NHL Board of Governors rejected the deal. The Board was led by nay votes from the Toronto Maple Leafs and Montreal Canadiens, who felt that adding three Canadian teams to the league would split up their market shares and give them less dominance on Hockey Night in Canada.

Angry fans in Winnipeg and Edmonton staged a boycott of Molson beer, as the brewery was the major sponsor of

Hockey Night in Canada and an owner of the Canadiens. Their pressure tactics were successful; in a new vote, Montreal switched sides (Toronto owner Harold Ballard remained obstinate) and gave the yeas enough votes to carry the merger through. With Gretzky on board, the Oilers made the playoffs in their very first NHL season. In 1980, Calgary would get another chance to compete with Edmonton. Nelson Skalbania, who, as the owner of the Indianapolis Racers, had sold Gretzky to Pocklington, gathered a group of investors with the aim of buying the struggling Atlanta Flames and moving them from Georgia to Calgary. The move was successful. Ironically, the Flames' first NHL game pitted them against the Nordiques, the same franchise which had faced the old Cowboys in one of the ugliest nights in pro hockey history. With the Flames established in Calgary and plans for a new arena in place, the stage was set for a new Battle of Alberta. The Flames and Oilers would soon forge a rivalry that would make Alberta the world's hotspot of hockey for a decade.

The Glory Years

If, back in 1979, you had asked Oiler fans who they thought was going to be their most hated National Hockey League rival, they probably would have guessed the Winnipeg Jets. After all, the Jets and the Oilers had contested the very last Avco World Championship Trophy final before leaving the dying World Hockey Association for the NHL. The two teams would now be competing to see which of the prairie WHA teams would be the quickest to make an impact in the NHL.

After just one NHL season, that all changed. Nelson Skalbania led a group of Calgary investors in the purchase off the struggling Atlanta Flames franchise. The Flames would move to the Calgary Corral in time for the 1980–81 season. The Corral held just 7,242 fans. It was a temporary home, and in 1983 the Flames moved to the Saddledome, built across the street from the Corral on the Stampede grounds. The Saddledome would be the centrepiece of Calgary's 1988 Olympics, hosting both the hockey and fig-ure skating competitions.

Skalbania and Edmonton Oilers owner Peter Pocklington were old acquaintances. Skalbania was once an investor in the Oilers back in the team's WHA days. He moved on to buy the Indianapolis Racers, where he signed 17-year-old phenom Wayne Gretzky to a pro contract before the teenager was eligible for the NHL draft. As a result of the Racers' poor showing at the gate, Skalbania was forced to put Gretzky on the market. Pocklington snapped him up in 1978, signing Gretzky to a personal services contract, not just a simple hockey contract, that tied up Gretzky's services off the ice as well as on it, and would prevent other teams from signing the man who would become the game's greatest player ever if the Oilers moved out of the WHA and into another league.

The Flames had been a competitive team in Atlanta. They had finished three games over the .500 mark in their last year in Georgia and had not missed the playoffs since 1975. The Oilers were quickly emerging as a new super-power. Gretzky would soon smash pretty well every NHL scoring record on the books. Paul Coffey, the fastest skater in the NHL, would break Bobby Orr's single-season records for scoring by a defenceman. Glenn Anderson and Mark Messier, two more lightning-quick skaters would both become reliable 50-goal scorers, and Messier would emerge as a fiery leader and the pre-eminent power forward the game had ever seen. In 1981, the Oilers would bring Jari Kurri over to Canada from Finland, and he would pair with Gretzky to create the most lethal goal-scoring combination in history. Kurri would go on to become the highest-scoring European-born player in league history. In 1982, future Hall of Famer Grant Fuhr made his debut in the Oilers goal; his ability to make spectacular stops and preserve leads gave the high-flying Oilers the freedom to execute coach Glen Sather's game plan to the fullest—attack, attack, attack.

The Oilers averaged over five goals a game, and reinvented the game in the 1980s, spurring an offensive explosion across the entire league. By 1983, just four seasons after coming into the NHL, the Oilers had made it to their first Stanley Cup final. By 1984, they had won their first Stanley Cup.

The Oilers presented a massive challenge for the Flames. Because Calgary was stuck in the Smythe Division with Edmonton, any chance the Flames had for extended postseason success required them to beat the Oilers. Their road to the Cup went through Edmonton. General manager Cliff Fletcher knew that he had to build his young Flames with one purpose: to try and counterbalance the Oilers.

"You always try to build your team to knock off the top team in the league," says Craig MacTavish, who played with the Oilers from 1986–94 and is the current head coach of the club. "With Cups in '84 and '85, the Oilers had established itself as the best team. So Calgary had to make it a goal for the team to knock off the Oilers."

With the Oilers providing the challenge, the Flames quickly went from a good NHL team to a great NHL club. Soon, Kent Nilsson had established himself as one of the top European forwards in the game, rattling off 100-point seasons as if they were easy. Lanny McDonald, the Alberta native son acquired from the Colorado Rockies in 1981–82, soon became the fan favourite and a 60-goal scorer for the Flames.

What really concerned Fletcher and the Flames more than anything was the Oilers' toughness. While history remembers the Oilers for their high-flying, high-scoring ways, the reason those players were free to score is because the Oilers opponents' knew bad things would happen to them if they tried any funny stuff with the Edmonton stars. Dave Semenko was quickly hailed as the top fighter in the game. In 1984, Kevin McClelland was brought in to give the Oilers a second top NHL enforcer. In 1986, Marty McSorley, yet another tough guy, was brought into the fold. The Oilers had toughness throughout their lineup; defencemen Don Jackson and Lee Fogolin were always willing to go, and Dave Hunter and Dave Lumley gave the Oilers a unit of crashers and bangers who were willing to win the ugly battles that come with every meaningful hockey game.

"That's the major difference between hockey now and how it was back then," says Bob Murdoch, who played with the Flames in their inaugural year in Calgary before moving behind the bench to become an assistant coach with the club. "If you decided that you were going to touch Gretzky, you would have to answer to 18 or 19 other Oilers."

While the Oilers continued to win, they gave the Flames all the motivation they needed to get better—and tougher. Tim Hunter became one of the top tough guys in the game, and he was joined by the likes of Paul Baxter—acquired from the Pittsburgh Penguins—and Neil Sheehy, a Harvard man who had boxed as an amateur. Jim Peplinski, who also had a knack for scoring key goals as well as being able to drop the gloves, gave the Flames their own unique style of power forward.

By 1984, the Flames were giving the Oilers a run for their

money, and there was no arguing that the best two teams in the NHL played in the same division and were fated to meet each other in the early rounds of the playoffs. Players on the other NHL teams began referring to Alberta as "Death Valley." Because of the proximity of the cities, teams would often play back-to-back (or two games in three nights) in the two Alberta cities, and consider themselves fortunate if they could scrape out a tie from the two games.

From 1983–90, each and every Stanley Cup featured a finalist from Alberta—either Calgary or Edmonton—with the Oilers winning five Cups over that span while the Flames knocked off the venerated Montreal Canadiens in 1989. If you ask the Flames and Oilers alumni, however, they will tell you that the toughest series they played in weren't the Cup finals, but the Battles of Alberta that were regular occurrences in playoffs from the mid-'80s to early '90s. A war between Edmonton and Calgary became an April tradition.

"When you think of it, it wasn't right at that time," says former Oiler Mike Krushelnyski, who would score 43 goals in his first season with the club and won Stanley Cups with the franchise in '85, '87 and '88. "We were the two best teams—and the two best teams should meet in the Stanley Cup finals." That opinion is shared by Charlie Huddy, Krushelnyski's former Oilers' teammate who was with the Oilers for all five of their Cups. "I think, with the style of hockey they played and with all the great players they had, from (Theoren) Fleury to players like (Joe) Nieuwendyk who came on down the line, I think if we would have been in different divisions that we would have met in at least a couple of Cup finals. I can't say how many of the five, but probably a bunch."

Whether it was the two cities' traditional rivalry with each other in everything else, the Flames' need to continually challenge the Oilers' toughness, or the NHL schedule, a hatred between the two teams was built that would fuel the most heated standoff in North American sport. Not only would Oilers and Flames fans be treated to great hockey, they would also see bloody brawls. The violence wasn't choreographed like it is in today's NHL, where the coach taps the designated fighter on the shoulder to take on the opposition's designated fighter when he feels the game needs a shot in the arm. No, the Flames and Oilers fought because they didn't like each other.

"We were just like the Hatfields and the McCoys," says former Oiler Dave Hunter, whose brother Mark played for the Flames after Dave was sent to Pittsburgh in 1987–88 after winning three Cups with the Oilers. "Mark said that if Calgary beat Edmonton, they knew they were on their way, and we knew if we beat Calgary we would be on our way to the Cup...It was always like, who's going to be the last man standing? If you're not going to fight 'em, you're going to have to outlast them."

"They had Marty McSorley, McClelland and Don Jackson, they had Dave Hunter and Dave Lumley, who competed like madmen," recalls former Flame Tim Hunter (no relation to Dave), who is now an assistant coach with the San Jose Sharks. "We had myself, Peplinski, Neil Sheehy and Baxter. If Sheehy even tried to do anything to Gretzky they would come at him, then later there was the great battles between Dave Brown, Stu Grimson and Jim Kyte. What made it special wasn't just the talent on the two teams, but the toughness on the two teams. We were both even when it came to tough enforcers."

"I just remember that the rivalry between us and Calgary was really unbelievable," says former Oilers enforcer McClelland, who earned 1,298 penalty minutes and four Stanley Cup rings as an Oiler from 1984–90. "There was so much intensity and so much battling. We really went to war. In the playoffs, role players like myself, Dave Brown, Dave Semenko and Marty McSorley, we would all have to wait until the next round to get a goal or an assist. Because we spent most of the Calgary series in the penalty box." This coming from a man who scored one of the biggest playoff goals in Oilers history. In Game 1 of the 1984 Stanley Cup final, McClelland scored the lone marker in the Oilers 1–0 whitewashing of the defending champion New York Islanders. That win on Long Island was the springboard to Edmonton's first championship.

McClelland says that, as a scrapper, he understood he had a job to do—and that was to pummel the Flames whenever he was called upon to do so. "It wasn't personal. Paul Baxter, who was one of Calgary's tough guys, was my good friend. We were together in Pittsburgh when I was starting off. He helped me a lot. We were friends off the ice. But as soon as he pulled on the Calgary uniform and went on the ice, we battled hard. Tim Hunter and myself, we battled and battled in game after game. One year, we did a photo shoot together for TransAlta (an Alberta utility) and we just laughed about things."

Hunter also remembers that shoot. It was a public service campaign warning contractors to call the utility before they dig, to make sure they didn't hit any live wires. The photographer had the two tough guys standing back to back and chest to chest. The picture ran with the slogan "Mess with electricity and it's lights out." Hunter recalls that it was fun, but he also remembers how it stung to be in the same room with McClelland, considering the Oilers had come off another Cup-winning campaign. "He had just won the Stanley Cup and I was jealous. He and I had a lot of battles."

McClelland recalls how the Oilers' fighters would actually work out on the bench who would take on which Flames tough guy. "But we did know about their guys. When they got (Neil) Sheehy he was a Gold Gloves guy at Harvard. I remember going to the game and asking Marty, 'who's going to try him first?' and things like, 'I'll try him first' and the other tough guy would say, 'I'll get him next.'

"I can remember one game that we cleared the benches. I had already got into two scraps in that game, and I was lying on the ice with Tim Hunter. Hunter and I were both on our sides and we were still throwing punches at each other. I still have that on tape and look back at it and wonder about just how crazy it was back then."

Hunter recalls that very battle, and he has a chuckle or two when he thinks back to it as well. "I've got the same video. I know someone who made a video that has a couple of hours of my fights on it. And there are about 90 per cent of the Flames/Oilers fights. And that fight is on there. It's the funniest thing you'd ever see, I don't think if we tried, that we could do it again. We were both so angry that we were still trying to fight when we were on our sides. It was a real fight to the finish."

Peplinski remembers that McClelland used to give Baxter fits. Baxter had been a fighting mentor of sorts for McClelland when the two had been teammates with the Pittsburgh Penguins. When the two ended up at opposite ends of the Calgary/Edmonton rivalry, Baxter was frustrated that McClelland had learned all too well, and knew pretty well all of his old teacher's moves. Peplinski says that during one brawl, Baxter, who was scrapping McClelland, yelled over to him. "He said, 'C'mon, let's trade.' Can you believe that? We traded fighters right in the middle of a brouhaha."

But while for McClelland it wasn't personal, for so many of the other Flames and Oilers, it was. There were so many great individual rivalries within the Battle of Alberta. Doug Risebrough, who would later go on to become coach and general manager of the Flames, was brought in from the Montreal Canadiens to help neutralize the Oilers' scoring. The Flames got big centre Joel Otto to act as a foil for Messier. Even faceoffs between the two became can't-miss TV.

"From our standpoint, my role was to neutralize him, to get him off his game," Otto says of his personal rivalry with Messier. "It was something that probably meant more to me. I'm sure he didn't think twice about playing against me. He was one of the toughest players you could ever play against. He was a mix of unbelievable skill and brute force...Those games are fun to relive now, but they weren't so much fun to play in."

MacTavish says that it was the clash of personalities between the two teams that made the Battle of Alberta such a compelling rivalry, and why there is nothing in today's NHL that can compare. "I think part of the reason there isn't a comparison is because of the match-ups between the teams. At that time, fighting wasn't the only part of the rivalry, but it was a major part of the rivalry. We had so many great match-ups between our tough guys and their tough guys. And whenever one team would have the advantage, the other would try and counter. When Theoren Fleury (the diminutive All-Star superpest and 100-point scorer who made his debut with the Flames in the season they won the Cup, '88–'89) first came in, we didn't have a player of that size who could answer the call, but when we got Mark Lamb...we noticed that...Fleury became a little more quiet."

Don Edwards, the former Buffalo Sabres great who came to Calgary in 1982 and participated in the Battle until 1985, remembers the pressure the Flames would put on themselves, that they each had to outshine their Oilers' foil in order to win games. "What made the Battle so interesting is that we both had such balance. We both had enforcers, goal scorers, defensive specialists and playmakers. We had all the ingredients to make up a good team... You had to deal with it as a player. And the rivalry was so personal from player to player, it put a lot of pressure on you. Because Gretzky was so good, Nilsson had to deal with the pressure that his line needed to outplay Gretzky's line on that night. Our attitude was 'If you weren't sore, you didn't care enough.' Heck, the exhibition games were just as bad."

Oilers Hall of Fame goaltender Grant Fuhr, the man who stoned the Flames on so many occasions, enjoyed a personal battle of his own with Flames' netminder Mike Vernon, who led his team to the Cup in '89. "I really enjoyed the rivalry, enjoyed playing against Calgary," recalls Fuhr. "I think Vernie and myself had a pretty good rivalry of our own, we had faced each other in junior and had carried that over."

Maybe a key reason the Battle became such a heated rivalry was the Flames' need to constantly prove themselves against the Oilers, and how they felt the Oilers were an arrogant bunch who had no problem running up the score against the Flames if they had the chance. The Flames wanted to show that they could stand up to the neighbourhood bully.

"It wasn't just a game. The rivalry was more than just the players. It was the owners, and the fans," says Murdoch. "And that was the thing with the Oilers. They liked to embarrass you. With a team like the Islanders, they beat you, but they didn't go out to embarrass you. But the Oilers were a lot like the Russians. They got more excited as they scored. So they wanted more and more goals...The Oilers were able to do two things: they were either able to bring out the best in you, or they would bring out the worst in you."

Murdoch can recall a game in his final year as a player when he challenged Semenko, and learned what it was like to take on the toughest fighter in the game at that time. "In one of my final years as a player, I got into it with Semenko. I always knew that when I played against him, I wanted to be physical. He was so big and strong, but I always wanted to hit him early in the game. Well, there was one game where I hit him early and he just beat the shit out of me. The linesman was holding me, and I wanted to get back at him. He said, 'Bob, if you keep going I will let you go—and he'll kill you.'"

Jamie Macoun spent a decade on the Flames blue line, winning a Cup in '89, before being sent along with star scorer Doug Gilmour to Toronto in a blockbuster deal that helped make the Maple Leafs a contender throughout the mid-'90s. He recalls how he would get butterflies before he played the Oilers. He didn't get those kind of nerves before a game against any other team. "I think the one thing that I will always remember is how nervous I used to get on the trip to Edmonton. On the flight, on the bus to the Coliseum, or just walking around in that arena, the tension was so high. I was just so nervous; the fear of making mistakes was so great, because the Oilers could score on you so much. The result of that is that when we went into Edmonton, we'd either play really well or play very poorly. There was no in-between. When you beat them, it was like winning the Cup all over again.

"For the fans and players, it was personal. Winning and losing to Edmonton, those results were more important to fans than any other games of the year. The city was always on the upswing when we beat Edmonton. The Battle of Alberta featured the best two teams of the late '80s. But what was a shame is that people from other NHL cities didn't get to see enough of it. Locally, every Battle game was on TV, but it wasn't always in the highlights in other places. Usually, the only times TV stations out east would show highlights from our games was when we had a bench brawl."

Of which there were more than a few! Macoun and former teammate Perry Berezan both recall their fair of share of donnybrooks. "My first game against the Oilers was in the Corral, and there was a bench brawl," remembers Macoun with a laugh. "Everyone just grabbed another player to start a tussle. And I got Semenko, and he started pounding me. What I tried to do was bury my head into his chest and throw punches inside. Then, he stopped punching me, so I thought I must have hurt him. But what had happened is that Pepper (Jim Peplinski) had grabbed him and they started tussling. The next day, I was talking to my parents on the phone, and they kept asking, 'How are you?' I kept telling them I was fine, and I asked them why they kept asking me that. They told me that in both the *Toronto Star* and *Sun* there was a picture of Semenko pounding me."

"I remember *Sports Illustrated* came to do a story on the Battle of Alberta," says Berezan. "We played our first game when they were doing this story, and I was on the ice to start the game with three of our toughest guys. Bob put Nick Fotiu, Neil Sheehy and Tim Hunter on the ice to start the game. So what is Sather supposed to do? He puts McSorley, McClelland and I think Semenko on the ice. We are 10 seconds in, and we are in a five-on-five brawl. We all got thrown out...they barely dropped the puck and we were squaring off!"

Kelly Buchberger, who made his Oiler debut in the 1987 playoffs and went on to captain the team from 1995–99, says that he can recall more than a few brawls. He thinks when it comes down to it, the rivalry wasn't about who won the fights, it was about who scored more goals after 60 minutes of hockey. "I remember more than a few five-on-fives. It's amazing to look back on those games and remember what happened. But I think when you get a little older, you get a little wiser. A lot of those brawls simply came out of the heat of the moment, and we were lucky that no one ever got really badly hurt. But we were never really going out there to fight; our goal against the Flames was always to try and get the two points. It's just when you play a divisional opponent so many times in a season, a lot of things will develop."

Despite all of the bad blood and brawls, players from both the Flames and Oilers will tell you that there was very little cheap stuff in the games. The games weren't plagued by the constant hooking and holding that mars today's NHL game. While there were a few controversial incidents, such as Mark Messier's brutal check on Mike Eaves in 1984 which left the Flames forward badly injured, both camps agree that the Battle would never have got to the point where fans would have had to see hits from behind or sticks to the head, the kind of dirty play that presents a constant problem to today's referees.

"A lot of what made it great rivalry was the respect between the two teams," says Dave Hunter. "It wasn't just about the bullying and the fighting. We always looked down the road at them and knew that they were a great team, too. We respected them. When we met in the playoffs, no matter how we finished in the standings, we always knew it was going to go seven games. Against different teams you might think that a series might only go four, but before we even started the series against Calgary, we knew it was going to go seven. It was always a great fight between the two teams."

"The games were always played with honour and integrity," says Peplinski. "The players took care of justice on the ice. Yes, there was fighting but there wasn't any hooking and holding. It was great hockey."

"I think, that despite how heated it was, we had respect for each other," says Krushelnyski. "I knew if I went out there and gave Doug Gilmour a cheap shot, Peplinski or Otto was coming over. The game was fair. As accelerated and intense as the play was, there weren't that many serious injuries, because there were never really any hitting-from-behinds or stick-swinging or anything like that. Each team knew what they had to do to win. You knew there weren't going to be easy games, that you would have to go into the corners and once you got there you were going to be stalked, held, kicked and punched."

Krushelnyski recalls a game where he went out to cover the Flames' point, Al MacInnis, the defenceman renowned for having the hardest shot in hockey. Krushelnyski was hit and left in a vulnerable position. Krushelnyski says that MacInnis saw that he was in a bad spot and passed on a shot, knowing it could have seriously injured Krushelnyski. "As heated a rivalry as it was, guys knew when to push, but they also knew when to lay off. He laid off the shot. He knew it wasn't the right thing to do."

Even though the Flames and Oilers were often seen as instruments of the deep divisions that existed between Edmonton and Calgary, the rivalry was something that people in both cities and across the entire province cherished. Hockey fans in each city knew exactly when and where the Flames and Oilers were scheduled to play next.

"I think the the first thing you have to say about the Alberta rivalry was that it was such a good thing for both cities, and so good for the NHL as a whole," says Lanny McDonald, who scored his first career goal in the Montreal Forum as a member of the Maple Leafs, so he knows a thing or two about rivalries. "You knew you weren't sup-posed to look ahead to games that were well ahead of you, but each year when the schedule came out we would look exactly when the Edmonton games were happening on the calendar...We had two outstanding teams, we always knew we were two of the favourites to go to the Stanley Cup. It was good hockey; if you earned a point, you know that you had to go through a war."

Glenn Hall, the former Edmonton Flyer and Hockey Hall of Fame all-time goaltending great, was the Flames goaltending coach when they won the Cup in '89, and he remembers the sense of excitement that filled Calgary when Edmonton came to town. "You always had a real good look at the schedule. If a guy wasn't healthy to play in the game tonight, you didn't worry about it, as long as he was healthy enough to play the game against Edmonton. You didn't think about the Edmonton games when they were next in the schedule. You thought about them two weeks ahead...At the time, people from Edmonton really disliked Calgary, and everyone knew that, but people in Edmonton were actually surprised to find out that people from Calgary didn't like them."

Hockey has a weird way of bringing players together. After the glory days of the '80s, many of the veteran Flames and Oilers found themselves in the strange position of be-ing teammates on new clubs. Macoun recalls how strange it was for him to look across the Toronto Maple Leafs dress-ing room and see Grant Fuhr and Glenn Anderson. "You couldn't bring yourself to like those guys," he says, even though he and the ex-Oilers soon became friends when wearing Leafs blue and white.

Otto had to undergo the same kind of reconditioning when he ended up sharing the same dressing room as MacTavish in Philadelphia. "You played so much against these guys, you got a real hatred for them. But when you play with them, you realize what good guys they are, and you try to understand what made you hate them so much."

Peplinski now owns a national car-leasing firm, and his management position requires him to spend a lot of time in Edmonton. Knowing how heated the rivalry used to be, he admits that he was nervous when he first opened his Edmonton office. "Put it this way: After I left the game I bought a business that had an office in Edmonton. And for the first six months, when I would meet clients for Edmonton or be in any kind of public place I would be expecting some kind of altercation. How silly is that? I had to totally change my thinking, that there are some good people in Edmonton. I had to change the way that my thinking had been conditioned by the rivalry."

But each and every Oiler and Flame agrees on one thing: that there is nothing in hockey, nor will there ever be, anything quite like the Battle of Alberta. "Playing in a Calgary/Edmonton game meant playing with bumps and bruises," says Charlie Huddy. "There were a lot of good feelings that we took out of the rivalry, but a lot of bad feelings, too."

Tim Hunter spent some time with the Quebec Nordiques after nearly a decade with the Flames. Going to La Belle Province gave him the chance to experience the famous Battle of Quebec between the Nordiques and the Canadiens firsthand. While he says it was a thrill to play in that rivalry, it would be tough to rate it with the Battle of Alberta. "There was such a general hate for Edmonton. If you went to get gas on a game day, you'd see someone at the gas station and they'd say to you something like, 'You have to kill Edmonton tonight! You'd better kill them!' When I was with the Canucks, the games against Edmonton were very different. I even played in Quebec City in their great rivalry against Montreal and it didn't even compare to the Battle of Alberta."

Dave Hunter says now that years have gone by since the heady days of the Flames/Oilers rivalry, he has an appreciation of what it has meant to the province as a whole. "You don't understand how great it was until you quit playing! I was playing at (Ottawa Senator) Wade Redden's golf tournament in Lloydminster. Doug Gilmour was there, so was Charlie Huddy. And people came up to us and said how much they loved watching us play, telling us 'those were great games, weren't they?' And people say that to me all the time."

In the mid-'90s, Hunter was part of an Oilers alumni team that took on a Flames alumni squad in Red Deer. While the game was put on for charity, Hunter recalls that it really bore no resemblance to most old-timers games, which are usually tepid affairs. "When the game started we were all out there to have fun. And even though there were no fights, by the time the third period came around we all wanted to battle each other as hard as we could. We just wanted to compete against each other. And that was a great thing." The saying in the Oilers' dressing room is "Once an Oiler, always an Oiler." The same could be said of the Flames.

Let the Battle Begin

While the Flames moved to Calgary in 1980 and were inserted into the Smythe Division alongside the Oilers, it wasn't until the spring of 1983 that the teams would meet in their first playoff series. The Oilers, a season after Wayne Gretzky's record-breaking 92-goal season, were trying to recover emotionally from being knocked out of the 1982 playoffs by the lowly Los Angeles Kings, a series that included the famous "Miracle on Manchester," when the Kings rallied from a 5–0 third-period deficit in Game 3 to beat the Oilers 6–5 in overtime.

The Oilers were a powerhouse in the 1982–83 season, and were viewed as a real threat to the current New York Islanders dynasty, which had won three Cups in a row. Gretzky's 71 goals paced an explosive offence that averaged more than five tallies per game. Mark Messier, Glenn Anderson and Finnish phenom Jari Kurri had contributed more than 40 goals each, while rearguard Paul Coffey chalked up a 96-point season, earning comparisons to the great Bobby Orr.

Meanwhile, the Flames, coached by "Badger" Bob

Johnson, were much more of a lunchpail crew. They finished the season two games under the .500 mark in their final season at the old 7,242-seat Corral before moving into the 20,000-seat-plus Saddledome for the 1983–84 season. There were some rays of hope; future Hall of Famer Lanny McDonald scored a franchise-high 66 goals, while the "Magic Man," Kent Nilsson, registered a team-high 104 points.

Hockey Night in Canada commentator Jim Robson described this series best. "We were expecting a barnburner, but Edmonton burned our barn." The first Battle of Alberta playoff was a non-event, save for the amount of records the Oilers set in pummelling the Flames. The Oilers scored 35 goals in their five-game series win, including a 10–2 thumping of the Flames at the Corral in Game 3 and a 9–1 shellacking in the clincher on Northlands ice. The 35 goals would set a new playoff record for the number of goals scored by one team in a series that lasted just five games. The Flames scored just 13 times.

The only bright spot for the Flames came in Game 4. Down three games to none, the home team rallied for a 6–5 win over the Oilers in the last-ever NHL game played at the old Corral. After decades of hosting the likes of the Stampeders, the Cowboys and the Flames, the old barn would give way to the Saddledome that was nearing completion just across the Calgary Stampede grounds.

The morning of Game 4, a desperate Johnson got Flames third-string netminder Marc D'Amour outfitted in Oilers gear for the team's pre-game skate. He got his team to try and fire as many pucks behind D'Amour as possible to try and build their badly damaged confidence. The gambit worked for only the one game.

This is how dominant the Oilers were in that 1983 series. Only one of the team's regular skaters, Dave Lumley, didn't get a point in the five games. Each and every one of the team's defencemen had points in the series. "The only times the Flames weren't sucking exhaust was when the clubs walked off the ice between periods," wrote future Hall of Fame hockey scribe Jim Matheson.[49] With such firepower in their possession, the Oilers cruised to the Stanley Cup final, where they were expected to present the stiffest opposition the three-time defending champion New York Islanders had ever faced. Instead, the Islanders veteran guile won out—by a long shot. The Islanders made their sweep of the Oilers look as easy as previous Cup wins against the likes of the Minnesota North Stars or Vancouver Canucks.

The Oilers returned in '83–'84 with a vengeance. Gretzky scored 87 times and added 118 assists, while Coffey registered 126 points. Both Glenn Anderson and Jari Kurri broke the 50–goal mark, while Mark Messier boasted a 101-point campaign.

The Oilers began the season in grand fashion by spoiling the opening night of the new Saddledome, the rink designed as the centrepiece of Calgary's 1988 Winter Olympics bid. The Oilers were the first road team to face the Flames at the new arena in regular season play—and on October 15, 1983, the Oilers sent the Calgary fans home unhappy as they triumphed over the Flames by a 4–3 count. Kurri scored the first goal in Saddledome history just 1:51 into the first period.

The two teams would meet again in the 1984 Smythe Division finals. This time, the Flames were marginally better than the season before, two games over .500. The Flames did not get the kind of stellar performances from McDonald and Nilsson that they had enjoyed in '82–'83. Instead, the team was blessed with a more balanced attack. Eddy Beers had 36 goals, McDonald netted 33, and Nilsson lit the lamp 31 times while Hakan Loob, Nilsson's Swedish countryman, burst onto the scene with a 30-goal campaign.

Still, with the gulf between the two teams as wide as ever—the Flames did not beat the Oilers at all during their eight regular season meetings—the experts all predicted that the 1984 series would end as quickly and miserably for the Flames as the '83 Smythe final. Surprisingly, the Flames would put up a valiant fight, taking the series to the limit. In fact, this was the series that would establish the Battle of Alberta as the pre-eminent rivalry in the NHL throughout the rest of the '80s.

It started off well enough; the Oilers won comfortably on Northlands ice by a 5–2 count in Game 1. The Oil managed to launch 55 shots at Flames goaltender Reggie Lemelin, who kept the score from reaching the ridiculous heights of the games played one playoff season before. But Oilers coach and general manager Glen Sather didn't relish the win. After the game, he went to the media, furious about what he thought was excessive stickwork by the Flames on his star players. This would set a pattern for the remainder of the series—whenever his team was questioned, he would change the topic to what he perceived as goon tactics by the Flames in order to take the heat off his charges.

In Game 1, Anderson had to go for stitches after a deep cut had been opened over his eye by a high stick from Flames checking forward Doug Risebrough, whom Johnson had brought to the Flames to check the Oilers' high-flying forwards. Sather promised to send video evidence of the stickwork to the league, saying that Risebrough had intentionally carved his 50-goal man. "You don't turn your stick over and hack a player in the face. Glenn could have lost his eye."[50] Nothing came of Sather's protests. The league told the Oilers that even if the video showed that Risebrough should be suspended, the NHL would not have time to act until after the Flames/Oilers series was completed.

Exasperated by his team's poor performance in Game 1, Johnson made four lineup changes before Game 2. He added toughness by pencilling in scrappers Tim Hunter and Neil Sheehy; he also added Dan Quinn, who had been the Flames best rookie of the season. But Johnson's stroke of genius was adding Carey Wilson, who came to the Flames after starring for the Canadian national team at the Winter Olympics in Sarajevo. Wilson would score the winner at 3:42 of overtime to shock the Edmonton crowd in Game 2. The 6–5 Flames win would break a winless streak of 16 games for Calgary against the Oilers, and would improve the Flames '83–'84 mark to 18 straight overtime games without a loss. While Calgary had a record that definitely put it into the "mediocre" category, the Flames were a deadly efficient team in the extra frame.

The Saddledome was sold out for Game 3. Even though the Flames outplayed the Oilers for long stretches of the game, two goals from Coffey and a winner from Jaroslav Pouzar gave the Oilers a 3–2 win. What made the loss all the tougher to take was that McDonald, who had scored 99 goals over the past two seasons, missed a wide open net to tie the game with less than 10 ticks left on the clock.

The Oilers won Game 4 by an easy 5–2 score, but allegations of foul play by the Flames were again number one on Sather's mind. "I think Calgary spent more time trying to maim our team than beat us," he raged after the game. "Their stick work bothered me. There's four or five seconds left in the game and Glenn Anderson takes a two-hander across the back. It doesn't take a lot of courage... If they get great deal of satisfaction out of hurting people, that's fine...we get satisfaction out of winning games, scoring more goals."[51]

Oiler Pat Conacher was in his first of a 16-year NHL career that would see him play for the New Jersey Devils, Los Angeles Kings, New York Islanders and, yes, the Flames. He says that Calgary realized that if they wanted to compete with the Oilers, they had to use goon tactics on Edmonton's best players. "I don't think anything I experienced in my career was like that rivalry. Maybe the rivalry between the Islanders and the Rangers. But I remember that the series we had with Calgary was ferocious. I think we were the best two teams in hockey, and if we had been in different divisions we would have ended up in the final. But I think what Calgary changed for the series in '84 was that they came in with a game plan that they were going to go after our best players. Guys like Jim Peplinski and Neil Sheehy were going after Gretzky and our best players. It really was the signal that we were entering a different era in the NHL. It used to be that there was honour amongst the tough guys, that tough guys would take on tough guys. And you knew if you did anything to anyone on the ice, you would have to answer the bell. But the Oilers had to stay disciplined, we couldn't let the Flames goad us into penalties. So the Flames were doing these things to us without paying the price. I guess there's no honour amongst thieves, but you have to do what you have to do to win."

Peplinski, one of the leaders of the Calgary team as well as one of the toughest power forwards, recalls that often the Battle of Alberta games were so much like wars, it was hard to believe that no player ever got critically injured during a game. He asserts that the foul play went both ways.

"I remember when Tim Hunter took a skate in the face from Mark Messier, and I have to say that it didn't look very accidental. Don't get me wrong; I have a lot of respect for Mark, but there's always been a question in my mind about that. After that, I really had to question the scale of the rivalry, because it was a war on ice. If the skate wasn't accidental, I can't hold it against Mark; that was the nature of the rivalry, that we were in a war out there and we were going to do whatever we had to."

"I remember that every year we went into Calgary, each game always had a different look," recalls Oilers defence- man Charlie Huddy, who won five Cups with the franchise and is now an assistant coach with the team. "It didn't matter if it was game five of the season or game 65; we al- ways saw them and the games were always intense."

While Sather complained about the refereeing and the lack of calls on all the hacking and whacking, Huddy says the games were actually made all that much better because referees used their judgment and let the iffy plays go. That's a big difference from the game today, where the two-refer- ee system can see each team get up to 10 powerplays per game. "Back then, the refs let us get away with so much stuff," recalls Huddy. "That has changed, now; the refs see and call everything. Back then, they let us play. And that helped create some of the great battles; like, for me, trying to clear big bodies like Peplinski and (Joel) Otto away from our net."

Oilers fans expected their team to wrap up the series in five games, as they did the year before. This time, the Flames would spoil the party. Quinn scored a goal and an assist to help the Flames to a 5–4 win at Northlands. It was the spark the Flames needed to snatch some needed momentum.

The Flames nursed a 4–3 Game 6 third-period lead in front of a suddenly rejuvenated packed house, but a face off in the Flames zone went awry. Both Risebrough and Messier slapped their sticks at the dropped puck, both made contact at the same time and the puck floated into the air and over Lemelin's shoulder into the Calgary goal. This fluke allowed the Oilers to tie the game and sent the game into overtime. But the Flames had that 18-game over-time streak going, and a rifle shot by McDonald over the shoulder of Oilers netminder Grant Fuhr was the stroke that turned what was supposed to be an Edmonton cake-walk into a one-game winner-take-all nailbiter.

Calgary Herald columnist Steve Simmons predicted the Flames would go all the way and win the series in seven. "Outside of Game 1, they have outplayed the Oilers."[52]

In Game 7, Sather decided to play a pre-game hunch and yanked Fuhr from the goal and put Andy Moog be-tween the Edmonton pipes. The move backfired. Calgary scored on three of their first eight shots before Sather put Fuhr back into the Oiler net. Luckily for the Oilers, those three goals weren't enough for the Flames to take the series. The Oilers managed to tie the game, but not before a huge second period gut check. Risebrough had been successful in getting Gretzky off his game, so Ken Linseman, known affectionately as "The Rat" throughout his long NHL career thanks to his pesky ways, took a run at the Flames veteran. The Oilers had lost the composure that Conacher said they worked so hard to maintain throughout the series.

"Our games were always a war," remembers Linseman. "I always enjoyed the pleasure of playing Peplinski, Hunter, Otto and even Randy Holt. I always took a good beating. But I will never forget that seventh game (with the score tied 3–3)...I crosschecked Risebrough. He had been on Gretzky, and I thought maybe if I did something I could get Gretzky some space. But when I was given a...penalty, my balls went into my throat. I was sitting in the box and I didn't want to look at our bench, my life was flashing before my eyes."

Al MacInnis gave the Flames a 4–3 second-period lead on the powerplay due to Linseman's lack of discipline. But Linseman atoned. "We then tied it up, and I ended up getting the winner."

Linseman batted the puck out of the air, before Lemelin could snatch it, and into the net to give the Oilers the 5–4 lead. He also fed Kurri with a perfect breakaway pass for the Oilers' sixth goal. These goals helped turn a gut wrenchingly tight game into a 7–4 laugher. McDonald says that after Linseman scored, Messier was the star of the third period, which the Oilers dominated. In many ways, this was the game that transformed the Moose from a great scorer on a great team to the icy leader who would glare at any team-mate he felt wasn't leaving it all out there on the ice. This was the game—and series—that transformed Messier from a great player into a surefire Hall of Fame legend.

"I remember that Game 7, and how Mark Messier took control of that game," says McDonald. "He was the best player on the ice in that third period and they eked out a victory." Messier's play wasn't without controversy. During those 1984 playoffs, he delivered one of the most memorable bodychecks in the history of the rivalry. He caught Flames forward Mike Eaves, who had a history of concussion problems, against the glass; the resulting crash not only concussed Eaves, but left him with a dislocated shoulder and broken wrist.

Don Edwards, the veteran goalie who split time with Lemelin in the Flames' cage and won Game 2 of the series, will never forget the Messier/Eaves incident. "I remember how tough the games in Edmonton were, especially the Mike Eaves hit. It was one of the dirtiest checks I had ever seen. Mike had a severe concussion. He was broken everywhere. Why was it so dirty? It was a charge. Messier skated about 35 feet to get to him and he left his feet when he hit him. Mike never had a chance. Messier went right at him and he sent Mike right into the dasher boards. Mike was defenceless; it was the most vicious thing I have ever seen in hockey."

Edwards says that he also remembers how Paul Reinhart, the Flames top offensive defenceman, but who had missed three quarters of the season due to injury, could also be heard screaming in pain as his cranky back acted up, and how he endured the pain so he wouldn't have to take himself out of the game. "In the same game as the Eaves hit, Paul Reinhart was being taken to the dressing room; he had really bad back spasms, and he was screaming. He could barely bear the pain in his back, but he wanted to play."

Peplinski says the Oilers should never have doubted Fuhr, who now is a member of the Hockey Hall of Fame. Fuhr was a clutch goalie in an era when scoring was at an all-time high and shutouts were rare. So, other than wins, it is hard to compare his career stats to the greats who came before, like Glenn Hall or Terry Sawchuk, or the greats who came after, like Martin Brodeur or Dominik Hasek. "I think he was one of the greatest goalies who ever played," Peplinski says of Fuhr. "Some people will talk about the number of goals he allowed, but you have to remember the only time he saw his teammates was when they skated back to the dressing room."

"As many good players as Edmonton has had, I don't feel enough has been said about Grant Fuhr," says Jamie Macoun, a mainstay on the Flames blue line for that series. "There would be games where we'd outshoot them 50 to 20 and they beat us 5–4. I think that Fuhr was one of the greatest goalies ever."

Unlike most goalies, Fuhr enjoyed the wide-open hockey. He enjoyed being called upon to make spectacular saves. He was never the kind of goalie who would complain that his defencemen weren't back to help him. He loved to see the goals go in at the other end of the ice. "It was just the system we played. We wanted to play a wide-open style. We wanted to trade chances with the other team. Calgary was a team that had some great offensive talent and they kind of liked to play it wide open as well, so it created a great rivalry and it was a lot of fun. And I knew the guys could score three, four or five goals for me. That's a huge cushion for the goaltender and it helped take the pressure off."

While most goalies would prefer today's defence-first hockey, the neutral-zone trap and the huge padding that allows them to keep their save percentages well above the .900 mark, Fuhr says he would rather play in a shootout— because they were a lot more fun. "Even for me, it was fun to play wide-open hockey."

While the scores in all seven games suggest that they were end-to-end affairs, remember that both teams featured some of the best offensive players in the game. If either Wayne Gretzky or Lanny McDonald got half a chance, the puck ended up in the back of the net. The high scores weren't indicative of the number of good chances in the games, they were indicative of how well each team converted its chances. Huddy says that games against the Flames were actually as close-checking as you would find in the run-and-gun '80s. "You always knew that a game against Calgary was going to be a physical battle, it was tough every night. Not always because there were going to be a million fights, but you always knew there was not going to be very much open ice out there against the Flames. If you got the puck, you had to get ready to get hit; there was not much stick checking in the Battle of Alberta."

Dave Hunter, Huddy's teammate in 1984 and one of the key ingredients on the Oilers energy line, isn't afraid to use the words "neutral zone trap" to describe the Flames style. "We were wide open. Lots of hits and scoring chances. But I still think Bob Johnson had them playing the trap. They deny it, but I still say they did, just like Montreal played the trap at the time. The trap has been around for a long time."

The Oilers would only lose one more game against the Minnesota North Stars and the Islanders on the way to the Cup. In 1983, when the Oilers got through the Flames with ease, they would go on to lose the final to the Islanders. In 1984, the Flames gave the Oilers all the trouble they could handle. That season, the Oilers vanquished the Isles in just five games to earn their first Cup. Huddy says the hard time the Oilers got from the Flames helped them elevate their level of play to the point where they could beat the Islanders. "Having to play Calgary early made us focus on playing hard throughout the playoffs, and it really helped set us up for our next series."

"They were probably the second-best team in hockey and we would often end up playing them in the first or the second round," says Fuhr. "The intensity between us was great. There were a lot of one-goal games, a lot of overtime games. Every series we played against them, no matter if it went four games or seven games, every game was good. We knew that if we wanted to get to the Cup, we needed to go through Calgary, so we would have a series early in the playoffs that was played with the same intensity as a final. And that would set us up for the rest of the play-offs. Sometimes we would get a first-round series against Winnipeg—another very good hockey team—Los Angeles or Vancouver. And that was like a warm-up series for us, to get ready to play Calgary. But, a lot of times, we would get Calgary right in the first round."

In 2005, Linseman returned to Calgary to take part in

the Esso 3-on-3 Hockey Classic, a day-long event where alumni from around the NHL play to raise money for charity. Linseman was assigned to play for the Boston Bruins alumni (he had played in Boston after his years as an Oiler) and was actually assigned to share the dressing room with the Calgary Flames alumni. The man who knocked the Flames out of the playoffs in 1984 went over to Peplinski. "I said, 'why don't you punch me in the head for old time's sake?'" laughed Linseman.

The Slashing of the Jersey

There have been some awfully strange incidents in the history of the Flames/Oilers rivalry, from Tim Hunter and Kevin McClelland scrapping while they were laying on the ice, to Oilers' coach Craig MacTavish ripping the felt tongue out of Flames' mascot Harvey the Hound during the 2002–03 season. But no incident was as strange as what happened the night of January 2, 1986. During yet another bitter Edmonton/Calgary tilt at the Saddledome, veteran Doug Risebrough did something that stands out as a singular achievement in a rivalry that has lasted well over two decades. Risebrough slashed and tore up Marty McSorley's jersey.

A melee erupted between the Flames and Oilers at 17:45 of the second period, in which the cagey veteran was mismatched against McSorley, one of the three Oilers heavyweights. Meanwhile, Flame Tim Hunter squared off against Oiler Dave Hunter, Oiler Kevin McClelland tangled with Flame Jim Peplinski, and veteran Edmonton defenceman Lee Fogolin got into the fray when he took on Calgary's Paul Baxter. McSorley lost his sweater in the skirmish; this was a common occurrence, as McSorley liked to shake free of as much equipment as possible so his arms would be free to inflict as much damage as they could. The NHL now has rules in place that force players to have their sweaters tied down. If a player's sweater comes off during a fight, he is now subject to a misconduct.

The brawl was a chance for the Flames to vent their frustration at the Oilers. The Flames had not beaten the Oilers all season long, and the Calgarians desperately wanted to do anything possible to slow Edmonton's momentum, as the Oilers were well on their way to the NHL's best record in the regular season.

Risebrough, who had been a Stanley Cup winner with the Montreal Canadiens before coming to the Flames, had become a real agitator for Calgary. He was often charged with the responsibility of being Wayne Gretzky's foil, and he had developed a nasty streak over the years. The Battles of Alberta brought out Risebrough's competitive nature, which he would carry on when he took over as the Flames' head coach—and later, general manager—in the early '90s.

McSorley's jersey lay on the ice after the linesmen and referee restored order. Before the Oiler could claim it, Risebrough, still in a rage, claimed the blue-and-orange sweater and took it to the Flames penalty box with him. Risebrough had no intention of returning the jersey; instead, he slashed it to pieces with his skate blades.

Anyone who has ever been around the Edmonton Oilers know that the team's players treat the team's crest and logo with almost a religious reverence. Walking on the Oilers logo on the carpet in the team's dressing room is frowned upon. Players who would dare toss their jersey casually into their stalls would be chastised. To have a Flame destroy a jersey was a high crime, indeed. In the second intermission, just minutes after the jersey slashing, Harvey the Hound jacked the crowd by tossing an Oilers doll around the ice.

In the aftermath of the incident, Oilers' general manager and coach Glen Sather threatened to send the Flames a $1,000 invoice to replace the torn jersey. "It costs $800 for the crest, $200 for the jersey."[53]

The Flames would not beat the Oilers until the final game of the '85–'86 season, a 9–3 romp that was punctuated by a huge line brawl that started the game. The two teams would meet for the third time in the post-season later that spring, and resulted in one of the most classic playoff series in the history of the NHL.

1986—Steve Smith and Sport Cola

When the 1985–86 season began, a strong majority of Oilers fans felt their team was pretty well predestined to three-peat as Stanley Cup champions. As the regular season wore on, the team gave every indication that they would repay their fans' faith in the spring of '86. The Oilers scored 426 goals over the regular season schedule, an average of well more than five a game. Defenceman Paul Coffey scored 48 goals, breaking Bobby Orr's record for goals in a season by a defenceman. Ten Oilers were selected to play at the NHL All-Star Game in Hartford. Wayne Gretzky had his greatest season ever in terms of points scored; he finished the season with an NHL-record 215. He also set the NHL record with 163 assists in a season. And the team earned 119 points, which gave it the new Presidents' Trophy, a new award created by the NHL for the team that finished first overall in the regular season standings.

Of course, with dominance came a certain arrogance. When visiting teams came to Northlands Coliseum, they were made to feel that they were definitely playing second fiddle to the greatest show on ice—the Oilers. While owner Peter Pocklington was spending millions on Wayne Gretzky's contract, he made sure the bottom line was strongly adhered to when it came to dressing room expenses—especially the visiting team. No team felt as bitter towards its treatment in Edmonton as the Calgary Flames.

"Edmonton was always an organization that was know for being frugal," recalls Tim Hunter, the most famous tough guy in Flames' history. "When we came to Edmonton, we would always have the cheapest tape and the cheapest supplies. And they gave us Sport Cola, it was all bullshit! When teams went on the road, the home teams would supply them with necessities like tape and stuff so we didn't have to lug it all on the road. But all we would get is crap in our dressing room when we came to Edmonton, so we had to start bringing our own stuff." Of course, they were also steamed with the knowledge that the Oilers got Coca-Cola in their rooms. The road teams were dealt discount soda, which Hunter adds was a "slap in the face." (Readers who wonder at athletes drinking cola should recall that this was before the more recent notion of "fitness" in pro sports. Hockey players were known to smoke between periods in this era.)

Jim Peplinski, a gritty forward who could provide key goals while not backing down from the battles that were common in the Calgary/Edmonton games, says the team's dressing-room treatment was all part of the gamesmanship. "They used to do things like that in Montreal," he laughs. "Sather played there, he picked it up there. It was all penny-ante stuff. The thing was that you didn't talk about it; you showed that it didn't bother you and then you would go out and play and try to drive them nuts."

Bob Murdoch, the former Flames player and an assistant coach with the team that season, says that it didn't take much to get the Flames going when they played Edmonton. Players would latch onto anything they perceived as subpar treatment and then use it as a motivational tool when they took the ice against the Oilers. "I think if those kind of things happened to us on the Island, we really wouldn't think anything of it. But because it was in Edmonton, we took it as an insult. After all, the Oilers exuded a certain arrogance. Sometimes they would give us bad equipment, or they would change our ice times; they would tell us we would have to go and practice out at the West Edmonton Mall rather than at the arena. But, as coaches, we could use those things as tools, to use those ploys as things that would motivate our players."

While Edmonton was tearing up the NHL, the Flames flirted with mediocrity for much of the campaign. Calgary finished the season nine games over .500 (a 40–31–9 record), 30 points behind Edmonton in the regular season standings. Edmonton skated away with the Smythe Division title with relative ease.

The divide between the teams was a given, but the rivalry was made all the more spicy by the deep political divide that had been created between the two cities. Calgary and Edmonton were going in opposite political directions. The provincial election of 1986 showed just how differently the two cities viewed the incumbent Progressive Conservative government.

Edmonton, the capital city that depended on government white collar, voted heavily in favour of the leftist New Democrats, a party which had always been associated with the notions of increased education spending and bigger government. Ray Martin's New Democrats captured 11 of the city's 17 seats in the vote, while the Tories could claim just four. In Calgary, the seat of big oil money and arguably the biggest booster of unfettered free enterprise of any city in Canada, the support stayed overwhelmingly with the Conservatives. While the New Democrats took the vote in the capital, Calgarians elected to stay the course with premier Don Getty. The Tories won in 15 out of the city's 18 ridings.

Calgarians began using a new nickname for Alberta's capital—in honour of the city's left-leaning vote, Calgary continued to bash its northern neighbour as "Redmonton," a place which was a liberal island in a sea of Tory Blue old-school values.

While pro athletes will often pass the buck when asked about the role that politics play in sports rivalries, claiming that sport and politics simply don't mix, tough-hitting Oilers defenceman Craig Muni admits that all of the Oilers were aware of the political differences between the two cities. "I think there are still great rivalries out there, but the thing about Calgary/Edmonton was that it was about more than just hockey," says Muni, who made his Oilers debut in 1986–87. "It was more than team versus team. It was city versus city, politician versus politician and business versus business."

When the playoffs began, both the Flames and Oilers dispatched of their first round opponents with relative ease. The Flames swept aside the Winnipeg Jets in three games, while the Oilers routed the Vancouver Canucks in three games, outscoring them by a whopping 17–5 margin over the course of the series. That set the stage for a Battle of Alberta Smythe Division Final. Still three rounds removed from the Stanley Cup final, hockey fans across Canada got prepared to watch what promised to be what could be the finest series of the 1986 playoffs.

The Flames may have only beaten the Oilers once in their eight meetings during the '85–'86 regular season campaign, but it was a comprehensive 9–3 victory at the Saddledome in Calgary's second-last game of the season, boosting the confidence of the men wearing the Flaming Cs as they headed into the playoffs. As well, there were rumours that Flames coach Bob Johnson, who was famed across the league for being one of the best minds in the world when it came down to breaking down the strengths and weaknesses of the opposition, had devised a written plan on what was needed to beat the Oilers. At least that's what was reported in the media. According to former Flame Perry Berezan, Johnson's famous notebook was more of a ruse than anything else. "It was just scribbles," says Berezan, an Edmonton native who was in his first full season with the Flames in '85–'86. "I remember that one of his famous notebooks was auctioned off for charity, and all it contained was lines and scribbles. It was nothing but scratch marks, that was all."

Murdoch says that the notebook didn't hold a full game plan. Instead, it allowed Johnson the chance to make reminders to himself during the course of the game. "He would note things he could refer back to, things that he saw as the game went on; he would keep track of goals and who was involved." As well, the notebook offered ready reminders to the coaching staff on how they wanted their team to handle certain situations, from penalty kills to power plays to defensive zone faceoffs. These are the kind of things that can be forgotten during a game as emotional and heated as a Battle of Alberta.

Johnson and Murdoch had indeed devised a plan that would mitigate the Oilers' superior talent. The Flames defenders would allow Coffey to carry the puck into the Calgary zone and wait for Oilers there. They figured that when the Oilers were faced with a team that laid in wait, they would be confused and try to beat the Flames in one-on-one battles. They were right. "It was like they waited until the end of the season to reveal their plan on how to beat the Oilers," recalls Berezan. "They used video to show us how Paul Coffey and Wayne Gretzky like to play when they had the puck and the way that they usually entered the zone."

"No question, right from the start of the season all we would talk about was beating Edmonton," recalls Flames enforcer Tim Hunter. "Our goal was to play better than they did and exploit their weaknesses. When we got Bob Johnson as coach, he really used video to help us exploit those weaknesses. They had great forwards, but they weren't perfect. They had a great goalie in Grant Fuhr, but he had weaknesses."

"We knew we had to have a good game plan to beat the Oilers, because they were so good," says Murdoch. Johnson and his coaching staff went across the Atlantic Ocean to find a strategy that might slow down the highest-scoring team in hockey history. In what was then Czechoslovakia, the national team had perfected a system North Americans would later come to know as the "left wing lock." Johnson

introduced the system to the Flames before the Oilers series, and the system would soon become popular throughout the NHL. It was the same system Scotty Bowman employed with the Detroit Red Wings when they won Stanley
Cups in 1997, 1998 and 2002.

"Bob Johnson was a master at analyzing the Oilers,"
recalls Murdoch. "He found that when Coffey wound up or
when Gretzky wanted to gain the offensive zone, they would
always cross the blue line on the right side, our left side.
So, Bob wanted our left winger to take away that space, a
system we had learned from the Czechs."

On top of being a master strategist, Johnson had a
knack for finding something trivial and using it as a motivator. Before the Flames were to face the Oilers, he tried to
sell his team on the power of…well…strawberries. "Bob had
read an article about how strawberries helped heal scar tis-
sue faster," recalls Berezan. "So he would tell us to eat the
strawberries, that we would hit the Oilers and we would be
stronger because we would have eaten the strawberries.
So, all the guys started eating the strawberries, some because they believed the strawberries would help and others
because they were showing they were part of the team effort—and who wouldn't want to have a few?"

Murdoch says that the key to preparing the Flames
for the series was to convince them that they could break
their recent history and beat the Oilers. "Over an 80-game
season, so much of a team's success is mental. You need
to believe that you can win a game even before a puck is
dropped. I used to say that a game is never won before a
puck is dropped, but sometimes they are lost. The key to

preparing the Flames was getting them to believe that they could beat the Oilers."

Johnson was famous for coining the phrase "It's a great day for hockey." Before coming to Calgary, "Badger" Bob coached the University of Wisconsin to three NCAA titles in 11 years. He went to the Pittsburgh Penguins in 1990, and led that team to a Stanley Cup before tragically succumbing to brain cancer in 1991.

Murdoch recalls that Johnson always had time to talk hockey with pretty well anyone; he didn't turn away anyone who he thought could offer him a little insight on how to improve his team. "Bob would go out every day and want to talk hockey," Murdoch recalls with a smile. "He would go out wearing a Flames jacket, Flames T-shirt, Flames cap, Flames sweat pants and even Flames socks. And he would go and walk the streets and talk to people like that. And he would come back and say, 'What a great town! What a great town this is! Everyone wants to talk hockey. Everyone is stopping me to talk about the Flames!' Well he went out there and advertised it!"

He is remembered as an outstanding ambassador of the game, except when it came to the Oilers. Berezan recalls that even the mention of the words "Edmonton" or "Oilers" would bring the Flames' master tactician to a boil. "Oiler fans are different from Flames fans in the sense that they hate the Flames every day of every year while the Flames fans take longer to build up the intensity. But it wasn't like that for Badger Bob. He had no problem hating the Oilers every day of the year."

In fact, both Johnson and Oilers coach and general

manager Glen Sather were good at using psychology on their teams and on their opponents. "I remember how Edmonton players and fans always hated the way that Bob would rub his nose and scribble in his notebook," says Berezan. "And Calgary always hated that smirk of Sather's. In fact, what Sather did was perfect. That smirk represented the arrogance of the Edmonton Oilers. Even if you were up by a goal or two, you would see that smirk and it said, 'So what if you're up? Do you know who we are?' It said that they knew they could beat you."

The Flames weren't above turning the Oilers' arrogance against them, however. In that earlier 9–3 loss to the Flames, Gretzky broke his own NHL record by registering his 213th point of the season. The Oilers, though, were incensed when the Saddledome's PA announcer refused to acknowledge the record. Sather fumed that the order to not acknowledge the Great One had come from the Flames' front office, and accused Calgary of having no class. That game also featured a nasty brawl just after the opening faceoff. The Flames had just acquired veteran tough guy Nick Fotiu, famous for his years as the New York Rangers' policeman. Johnson tossed Fotiu out to begin the game along with Harvard boxer Neil Sheehy, who racked up 271 penalty minutes and specialized in driving Gretzky nuts. Some old friends from Edmonton were featured in Sather's opening lineup.

"I remember a game where we put Sheehy at centre and had Nick Fotiu and Hunter also out there," smiles Murdoch. "I think we had Macoun out there, too. And they had McClelland, McSorley and I think Semenko out against us. I remember Fotiu looked back at the bench and said,

'Well, boys, we all know why we're here. We might as well get at it.'"

Despite the 30-point gap between the Flames and Oilers in the regular season standings, the Smythe Final would be remembered as not only one of the greatest Battles of Alberta, but one of the best playoff series in the history of the league. The Flames showed that their late-season 9–3 win was no fluke; they dominated the Oilers in the first game of the series, winning 4–1. Future Hall of Famer Lanny McDonald scored just 1:27 after the drop of the puck, and it set the stage for a full three periods of Flames domination. When hulking Flames centre Joel Otto scrapped Oilers tough guy Dave Semenko in the first period, the boys in red showed that they weren't going to give any quarter when it came to the physical aspect of the game.

As time wound down in Game 2 of the series, the Oilers fans nursed a serious case of nerves. At the end of regulation time, the Flames had played the Oilers to a 5–5 tie (thanks to a Joe Mullen game-tying goal with 20 seconds left in regulation) in a game that showed off the offensive power that was apparent on both sides. Could the Flames squeak out an overtime winner—and take a shocking two-games-to-none lead in the series? The Northlands crowd let out a collective sigh of relief just over a minute after the puck was dropped to start the overtime frame. Glenn Anderson, who would go on to become the Oilers' all-time leader in overtime goals, beat Flames goaltender Mike Vernon to tie the series.

Two games into the series, the 30-point gap between the teams was forgotten. The teams travelled south to the Saddledome for the next two games. The Oilers, despite the emotional overtime victory, showed no carryover into Game 3. Edmonton was absolutely smothered by Calgary's tenacious checking. The Flames won by a 3–2 count thanks to a third-period winner from Otto, but the scoreline was deceptive. The Flames badly outshot the Oilers by a 38–19 count.

To be fair, those shot totals need to be taken with a grain of salt. Murdoch says the Flames knew all too well that the Oilers didn't mind giving up a lot of shots. They knew that in Grant Fuhr they had the best goaltender in the NHL between the pipes—and Edmonton wanted to lure the opposition into a game in which they traded chances. The Oilers were willing to give up a couple of odd-man rushes and decent scoring chances because it would open up the ice and create the room the likes of Gretzky, Kurri, Anderson and Messier needed to score.

"The one thing the Oilers were better at than any other team was their finishing," recalls Murdoch. "You could outchance them in a game 26 to 17 and they would beat you 8–2. We knew that all too well in Calgary, that if they got a good scoring chance they were likely to convert. What you had to do is go out and play a control game, to not try and go up and down too much, maybe kind of a boring game with a lot of stoppages. The Oilers didn't care how they beat you; if they needed to, they could win 3–1, but they were happy to beat you 9–7 or 7–5. If you looked at stats that the coaches like to look at, things like puck possession, zone time and scoring opportunities, there were a lot of times that we did better in those areas than the Oilers, but they were just so good at finishing that it didn't always matter that much."

Dave Lumley, who had scored the empty-net marker that sealed the Oilers' first Stanley Cup but had been benched for almost two full months before Game 2 of the series, was clearly frustrated by his team's lack of focus. "Everybody keeps saying they (the Flames) can't play any better," Lumley told the *Edmonton Journal.* "Well, they don't have to. They've beaten us twice. We've only had the lead for two minutes in the three games. That's hardly our style."[54]

Game 4 saw the Oilers come out with a 7–4 win. With seven goals to the road team, it would be easy to surmise that the Oilers' vaunted offence finally put itself into high gear, but that's not entirely the truth. Vernon, who had not yet shown any rookie nerves in the series, endured his worst game of the playoffs. The Flames actually outshot the Oilers 40–27, but Gretzky's hat trick provided the impetus for Edmonton in a fight-filled contest. Both Tim Hunter and Oiler Semenko—two combatants who were only too familiar with each other after a season's worth of battles—were tossed after a first-period tilt. In the third period, when it was obvious that the Oilers would win, Flame tough guy Nick Fotiu also got tossed after a melee, and Oiler Marty McSorley and Peplinski were also tagged with misconducts.

After four games, the series was not only tied 2–2, but each team had scored 16 goals.

Calgary went to Edmonton in Game 5 and repeated their performance of Game 1, coming out with a 4–1 win. McDonald and Otto scored second-period goals to turn what had been a 1–1 game on its ear. The Flames would return to the Saddledome to end the series and send the two-time champions back to Edmonton wondering what went wrong.

The Flames could not believe the reception they got when they returned to Calgary. Fans jammed the Calgary International Airport to welcome the team after the short flight south, and their support only fuelled the belief in the Flames that they could pull off the upset. Johnson had wanted his team to believe that they could beat the scariest team in hockey. At this stage, there was not one single doubter on the team. "I just remember that the Calgary Airport was just absolutely jammed," reminisces Otto. "The city was just so hungry for success against Edmonton. It really gave us perspective on what the series meant to the city. We couldn't move in the airport."

The Saddledome faithful—the majority of them clad in red in support of their Flames—got what they wanted in the opening stages of the game. The Flames jumped out to a 2–0 lead and looked good to pull off the upset on home ice. But the Oilers came back with five unanswered goals. Anderson supplied yet another winning goal and Edmonton quieted the Calgary fans with a 5–2 win. Unlike the Oilers' last win in Calgary, there would be no blame assigned to Vernon. After falling down by two, the Oilers showed the mettle which had made them champions the previous two seasons. At the end of the game, the Oilers outshot the Flames by a 39–24 count.

Entering Game 7, each team had won two out of three on the road, a fact that fed the Flames' confidence. Even though they had blown the chance to wrap up the series at home, they had played the Oilers even through six games. Both teams had scored 22 goals each in the previous six games.

In the third period of Game 7, neither team was going to blink. The game was tied 2–2, and an eerie silence had come over Northlands Coliseum. At no time over the past three seasons had any team given the Oilers so much trouble. Goals from Hakan Loob, the Swedish star who had scored 31 times during the regular season, and Peplinski had actually given the Flames a shocking 2–0 lead. Even though goals from Anderson and Mark Messier had tied the score, their efforts did not inspire confidence in the fans in attendance at Northlands Coliseum. The Flames also lost Gary Suter—their best defenceman in the series—to a knee injury after he was belted by Messier, but they did not despair.

The fans did erupt as Mark Napier led an early third-period rush down into the Flames' end, but Vernon, moving to his right, pushed the shot into the corner—it was a great save that would set up a bizarre series of events. Flames forward Berezan—who grew up in Edmonton and was a self-confessed Oilers fan before he became a Flame—ended up with the puck and skated it up the right wing. Berezan dumped the puck into the Oilers' zone, and it slid behind the net. Oiler Steve Smith, who was in his first NHL post-season, moved from behind the net and intended to throw a cross-ice pass right through Grant Fuhr's goal crease. The pass struck Fuhr's skate and bounced into the Oilers' net. Smith collapsed on the ice; he would not be celebrating his 23rd birthday with a victory. Instead, tears streamed down his face.

It was the kind of mistake that is vilified in sport, like Bill Buckner's famous muff of a ground ball that cost the Boston Red Sox a World Series in 1986, or how Leon

McQuay's fumble thwarted the Toronto Argonauts' final drive in the 1971 Grey Cup.

"I think I am the only man in history to score a series-winning goal from the bench," says Berezan. "I had dumped the puck into the Edmonton zone when I was in front of my own bench, and I didn't even see it go in. I remember how strange it was on the bench when the goal was scored. It was quiet. We were asking, 'what just happened?' and guys were saying, 'Steve Smith bounced the puck off of Fuhr. It's a goal!' We were facing off at centre after the goal and were still wondering what just happened. There was really no celebrating; we thought, okay, we're now up by a goal, let's take care of business."

Joe Mullen, the New York City-born Hall of Famer who would win a Cup with Calgary in '89 before moving onto the Pittsburgh Penguins, where he won two more, was in his first season with the Flames. He recalls that no one on the bench really had a good view of what was going on. "The light went on, but you didn't know what was happening. I remember that our bench was way down on the other end of the ice, far away from the goal."

While Berezan was an Edmontonian, after a year in Calgary he had no mixed emotions when he scored the goal. All of his old allegiances to the Oilers were long dead. "I grew up in Edmonton, and the one thing I was concerned about when I was picked by the Flames is how I would adjust mentally to playing for them. I grew up cheering a couple of Stanley Cup wins for the Oilers and I cheered for them in their old WHA days. So, coming to Calgary, I thought it might take me a little time to build up a hate for the Oilers. In fact, it took no time at all."

The Oilers had more than half of the third period left to tie the game (Smith's gaffe came with 14:46 left in the third), but their offence could not put a puck past Vernon.

Even though Smith was on the front page of newspapers across Canada the next morning, the Flames' game plan deserved more credit than it got at the time. The Flames won thanks to a fluke goal, but the Flames held the Oilers to just six shots on goal in the third period. Considering that the Oilers would have been desperate for the tying marker, six measly shots was an unacceptable number for Edmonton fans. As well, the Flames held the Oilers to just four shots in the first period of Game 7. Smith may forever be remembered as The Goat, but Johnson showed that his secret game plan to beat the Oilers was well thought out—and he had a team that executed it to the letter.

The Flames had won the series in seven, outscoring the Oilers 25–24. The elation was clear in the Flames' dressing room.

"This isn't for just for Calgary," bellowed an ecstatic McDonald to reporters. "This is for everybody. This is for the oilmen, this is for the oldtimers, this is for the wizened kids. To know you've knocked off the Stanley Cup champions. Yeah, it's fabulous."[55] In the present, McDonald still can look back and marvel at the '86 series. "Our goal was to find a way to get the series to seven games. But today, it is rarely even mentioned just how close a series it was. It was outstanding. It was entertaining. We knew we were a very good road team, and even though we had lost Game 6 at home, we were confident we could win Game 7 on the road. Our team that year was a great team. We knew we could skate with anybody. We had the kind of team where if you wanted to play rough, we could play rough."

Ironically, both McDonald and Gretzky are now executives with Hockey Canada, and they are often seen sharing a laugh or discussing team issues when a Canadian national team is either playing or practicing. McDonald admits that he and the Great One sometimes reminisce about hockey's greatest rivalry, and they have nothing but admiration for each other. McDonald also counts Sather as a friend, as the two have worked at hockey schools together in the past.

Cliff Fletcher, the general manager who built that Flames squad, recalls that the joy of beating the Oilers spread through the entire organization. Ever since the Flames moved to Calgary, the franchise had felt like David to Edmonton's Goliath. For the better part of a decade, Fletcher had built the Flames with one goal in mind: to eventually beat the Oilers. Finally, that dream had been realized. "The Oilers were a dynasty, and we woke up in 1982 and knew that the task at hand was going to be to try and catch up to them. Every day we would ask ourselves, can we get closer to the Oilers? Part of our motivation was out of fright; they were such a good team. And we knew we had a long way to go back in 1982. Then, we played in a couple of playoff series with them and lost, but by '86 we felt we had built a pretty good hockey team...All I remember was a sense of elation. I was just so proud of what our players did on the ice. We knew we had beaten the best team in history."

As the Flames celebrated, the Oilers' shock turned to despair. Dave Hunter recalls that after the shock of losing wore off, it was replaced by pain—not just emotional pain, but physical pain. "I remember getting out of bed a lot of mornings and being so sore. I was a third liner, one of the bangers. While some guys would skate and fight, we were always into body contact. There were great hits...Funny thing is, if you won the night before, you didn't feel sore. If you lost, then you were really sore. After losing in '86, we all felt real sore after that."

After the game was over, Sather ventured into the Flames' dressing room to congratulate the Calgarians. When the Oilers shocked the Montreal Canadiens in the first round of the 1981 playoffs, the Canadiens' brass made sure to congratulate Sather and his charges. That was the Montreal way, classy in victory, classy in defeat. Now, the tables were turned and Sather walked into the underdog's dressing room and uttered congratulations through gritted teeth.

Tim Hunter says that at first, many of the Flames were not sure of Sather's sincerity. "And it was satisfying. We had seen Glen Sather smirking on the bench, and the way he looked at us. And the team was as cocky as he was, they all had that swagger." Hunter was so suspicious, he made sure to look Sather right in the eye—and was finally satisfied that the salutations the Flames received from the Oilers' boss were indeed sincere.

After Sather finished, there was an awkward moment in the Flames' dressing room. There really was no way Sather could have made a graceful exit. One Flame could not re- sist the opportunity to unleash a barb in Sather's direction. Hunter recalls: "And I remember once Sather has finished congratulating us, you could hear one voice in our dressing room saying, 'Hey, Slats, want a Sport Cola?'...I don't know who said it, but it was priceless!"

The Flames went on to beat the St. Louis Blues in the Campbell Conference Final and were favoured to beat the Montreal Canadiens in the Stanley Cup series. But the Habs, fuelled by the Conn Smythe-worthy goaltending of rookie Patrick Roy, shocked the Flames in five games.

The turning point of the final came in Game 2. The Flames had won the first game 5–2 in front of the Saddledome faithful, and wanted to return to Montreal with a stranglehold on the series. The Flames did not find the Canadiens' defence as pliable in Game 2 as it had been in Game 1; the teams finished three periods tied 2–2. The Flames knew that one goal would give them a two-game advantage. But before many of the crowd had made it back to their seats following the break, Brian Skrudland made history. Scoring just nine seconds into overtime, Skrudland set a record for the fastest OT winner in the history of the playoffs. More importantly, the goal tied the series.

The Canadiens, who had won 22 Cups before this final, ballooned with confidence after the goal. It was as if that one moment signaled to the Habs that the ghosts of Canadiens teams past were indeed behind them, and would not allow them to lose. Montreal won the next two games on Forum ice, including a 1–0 shutout win for Roy in Game 4, and never allowed the Flames the chance to recover. The Flames lost the Cup on home ice.

Hunter, even though he won a Cup with the Flames in 1989, regards the '86 Cup final as The One That Got Away. "We should have won that one."

Murdoch, the Flames' assistant coach that season, is

more philosophical about why the Flames lost to the Habs. "Each year, our goal wasn't to win the Stanley Cup. Our goal was to beat the Edmonton Oilers. We knew that if we beat the Oilers, then we could win the Stanley Cup. There were so many highs in that series with the Oilers; it took so much out of us. That year, beating the Oilers, that was our Stanley Cup. It took us seven games to beat the Blues, and when it came time to play the Canadiens in the final, we had nothing left in the tank."

Murdoch says the Flames' failure to win the Cup that season mirrored the aftermath of many Oiler/Flames games. He recalls that most NHL teams were happiest to get the Flames and Oilers on their schedules after the two Alberta powers had played each other. "If you would look at both our records in games after we had played each other, I bet you they wouldn't be very good. I know that when the two teams played, you were left totally wasted. After you played the Oilers, you were totally exhausted, physically and mentally."

Because the Flames didn't win the Stanley Cup, Oilers fans scoffed that Calgary had only beaten their team because of a lucky bounce. It's a charge that is still levelled at the Flames by today's Oilers fans. But fans need to remember that it wasn't as if the Oilers had badly outplayed the Flames in the series. If that Smith incident had never happened, there was no guarantee that it would have been the Oilers, not the Flames, who would have scored the next goal. Considering how closely the series had been played, the game was still very much up for grabs—and if it would have gone into overtime tied 2–2, who's to say who would have scored the magical winner?

The Flames of '86 deserve far more respect than history shows them.

"For years we had been trying to compete against them," says Tim Hunter. "It was his (Steve Smith's) birthday, and I remember him crying on the ice. Yes, people said we won on a lucky bounce. But we put ourselves in that position that we could win on a lucky bounce."

"I feel really sorry for Steve," says Peplinski. "I think what happened to him is the kind of thing that could have happened to anybody. It turned out that he had a great career, he was actually one hell of a defenceman. What I think though is that the goal overshadows what was one heck of a series—from an Edmonton perspective, as well. That hockey was as good as anyone will ever see."

Winning that series would make Berezan very unpopular with his old Edmonton buddies. He returned to his hometown in the summer, and was not surprised to find out that the mother of one of his best friends would no longer speak to him. "I respect that," he laughs. "Edmonton fans are very loyal."

The Spear and the Sweep

The Oilers recovered from the shock of their 1986 upset at the hands of the Flames in the best way possible; they won 50 games in the 1986–87 regular season and won the Stanley Cup final over the Philadelphia Flyers in seven thrilling games.

The regular season of 1986–87 showed that the Flames had used the 1986 upset as a building block. The team finished 46–31–3, finally shedding the image of a team that was regularly flirting with .500. Together with the Oilers, they made the Smythe Division the toughest in all of hockey. American star Joe Mullen scored 47 times, while Al MacInnis chipped in with 76 points off the blueline and continued to show off his terrifying 100-mph-plus slapshot. But the Flames, who were the Cinderella story in the West just a year before, fizzled in the playoffs. They were eliminated by the Winnipeg Jets in a shocking first-round upset and never got the chance to meet the Oilers to decide the Smythe Division title.

In 1988, the Battle of Alberta, playoff edition, would be resumed. The Oilers, winners of the Stanley Cup three out of the last four seasons, found themselves underdogs on many of the pundits' prediction papers. Now under the tutelage of new coach Terry Crisp—a straight-shooting ice general who had learned to be as mean as he needed to be when he won two Stanley Cups as a member of the Philadelphia Flyers in their Broad Street Bullies days—the Flames finished ahead of the Oilers in the regular season standings. The Oilers may have been defending champs, but the Flames had earned 105 points in the '87–'88 regular season schedule compared to the Oil's 99 points.

The Flames were lead by Hakan Loob, the first-ever Swedish player to hit the 50-goal plateau in NHL history. Joe Nieuwendyk became just the second player in the history to score 50 goals in his rookie NHL season, joining New York Islanders' legend Mike Bossy in that select group. The Flames actually had a more potent offence than the Oilers in 1987–88; they scored 397 goals compared to the Oilers' 363. The Flames would not make a first-round playoff slip like they had in 1987. They disposed of the Los Angeles Kings in five games, setting up a Smythe Division final against the Oilers, who had easily disposed of the Winnipeg Jets.

The Oilers were a team that had changed significantly from their first three Cup wins. Gone was Paul Coffey, the slick skating defenceman who had broken Bobby Orr's single-season record for goals by a rearguard. Coffey, who was tired of the disrespect he felt was shown to him by Oilers coach and general manager Glen Sather, did not report to training camp at the start of the '87–'88 season. "The one guy who doesn't get talked about enough is Coffey," says Dave Hunter, who won three Cups with the Oilers. "He moved the puck to the other guys." When it became all too clear that the impasse between the all-star defenceman and the team would not be breached, the Oilers traded Coffey's rights to the Pittsburgh Penguins for Craig Simpson, a top prospect from London, Ontario. Simpson immediately clicked with the great Oilers' offensive machine. Simpson achieved a rare NHL feat that season, a 56-goal campaign in a season where he split time between two clubs.

Even though Simpson was new to the Oilers, he didn't need anyone to tell him how important the rivalry with the Flames was to his new team. "Everyone who followed hockey knew about the rivalry; you didn't need an introduction when you got involved in it. To compete at that level, we knew that we would have to give that little bit more when we would play Calgary, especially in a playoff series. As a player, you didn't need to say much about it. From the first or second shift in, you knew that you were going to have to give that little bit extra, that you were going to be asked to give or take that extra hit or make that extra play. You knew that when you played Calgary, you were always going to have to give more."

Dave Semenko, who had been traded to the Hartford Whalers, would no longer be lending his toughness to the Battle of Alberta. The NHL instituted a new crackdown on penalties in the playoffs, urging referees not to put the whistles in their pockets in the post-season as was the norm. The promise of increased penalties and the loss of "Sammy" lowered the temperature on the rivalry.

Still, the entire province was geared to see a battle between the Cup champs and the division champs, with the Oilers in the rare position of underdog.

Both teams had nearly a week off before the series began, which gave the media plenty of time to fuel the hype machine. Nieuwendyk tried to escape to the Rockies for a couple of days to get some rest and to get away from the pressure. But his trip to Lake Louise had just the opposite effect. "You can't get away," an exasperated Nieuwendyk told reporters after his trip. "Everywhere you go, there's hockey. Up in Lake Louise, all the skiers coming down the hill were either in an Oilers' sweater or a Flames' sweater."[56]

The penalty crackdown turned out to have a major effect on the first two games of the series. The Oilers' Game 1 win at the Saddledome, a 3–1 score decided in the third period by a goal from Jari Kurri and a breakaway marker from Gretzky, was maybe one of the most mundane post-season encounters ever held between the two teams. Flames fans were upset by the result; the bloodlust that was usually a given between the clubs never manifested itself. Still, Gretzky considered it one of the most important wins in Oilers franchise history. As underdogs, he felt it was vital that Edmonton draw first blood in the series. The Great One once again showed why he was not only a legendary player, but a legendary captain. He was a key part of the third period rally despite battling a bad case of the flu.

While the second game produced little in the way of fisticuffs, it produced a heck of a lot more in terms of drama. The Flames held a 3–1 second-period lead and looked good to even the series. But the Oilers erased the lead and the "C of Red" that filled the Saddledome worried that the home team could actually drop both of its home games.

In the third, Tim Hunter looked to be the unlikely hero. With the penalty crackdown making his fists less important than they had been in the past, his go-ahead goal showed that he still wanted to be a factor in the series. With less than four minutes left, however, Kurri buried a 25-foot shot past Mike Vernon, and the game went to overtime. Six minutes into the extra frame, the penalty crackdown became a large factor. Before the '88 playoffs, the post-season rule of thumb was that it would take a player lying dead on the ice to cause a penalty to be called in overtime. But Mark Messier was sent to the box, and Calgary fans anticipated a victory. The Flames boasted the top powerplay in the league. With MacInnis manning the point, Calgary enjoyed a 28.5 per cent success rate with the man advantage during the regular season.

Then came the great plot twist. Despite being down a man, Kurri was able to poke the puck up the boards, where Gretzky skated onto the puck at full stride. Instead of trying a deke or trying to slow up the play for one of his famous no-look passes, the Great One walked into a slapshot. He could not have placed it better. Vernon flailed at it with his glove, but the puck had already hit the roof of the net, just underneath the crossbar.

Kelly Buchberger says that Gretzky's overtime winner has got to be the greatest goal in the history of the Battle. "The biggest one is the goal Gretzky scored under the bar in overtime. That goal really stood out, separating two teams that were very even going into that series. That was the shot the Oilers needed to help spur us to win another Cup." Gretzky still calls that shorthanded game winner the greatest goal he has ever scored.

Bob Murdoch compares the way the Oilers killed penalties to how the Montreal Canadiens approached playing a man down when he was part of that franchise under Scotty Bowman's reign in the '70s. "When I played in Montreal, Scotty Bowman would always put Frank Mahovlich out on the penalty kill, and he would just hang out by the red line. But what happened is that the two defencemen who were supposed to be on the point would get so worried, they would back off, and that would create a three-on-three in our own end. The Oilers were the same way, you were so worried that Gretzky would score on you."

According to Craig MacTavish, the current coach of the Oilers and a winner of three Cups with the dynasty, Calgary fans should never have been surprised with the Oilers' success in the Saddledome. He says that some of the great defining moments in the history of the Oilers franchise can be traced to Calgary. "I think some of the most historic team meetings in the history of the Edmonton Oilers occurred in the Calgary dressing room. I can't specifically say what happened at those meetings, but they really were historic. Those battles between Calgary and Edmonton were battles between the best two teams in the league, and we were the two top teams for quite a long period through the '80s."

The refereeing style remained a hot topic for Game 3, but for radically different reasons. The story was not the crackdown, but a non-whistle which still infuriates Flames fans to this day. The Flames, desperate to try and get back into the series, were tied 1–1 with the Oilers in the second period of Game 3, setting up a chain of events that will always be remembered as one of the low points in the history of the Battle.

At 8:54 of the second, Flames forward Mike Bullard— who had enjoyed a 103-point season—prepared to jump on the ice for his next shift. Meanwhile, Oilers tough guy Marty McSorley, a former teammate of Bullard's in Pittsburgh, was cranked by a thunderous bodycheck from Gary Roberts, a young power forward who would become one of the most hated men in Edmonton in the later years of the battle. McSorley, dazed, skated to the bench, and struck out at the next skater in a red jersey that he saw. That was Bullard, who had just hopped on the ice from the Flames bench.

What happened next is not a safe topic for a Flames fan and an Oilers fan to argue over when they've had a few beers. Flames fans will recall that McSorley skewered Bullard with his stick, leaving the injured forward crumpled on the ice. Oilers fans will say that the stick contact was minimal or even that McSorley never made contact with Bullard. They claim that the Flames forward, sensing he could get his team a powerplay, gave a performance worthy of an Oscar as he faked an injury.

Even though the linesmen saw the infraction and were going to advise that a major penalty be called, they did not have the power to stop the game. With Bullard curled up in the fetal position near the Flames bench, Charlie Huddy scored the go-ahead goal for the Oilers. As soon as the red goal light flashed, the linesmen advised the referee that a penalty should be called. McSorley was given a major, but because play was not halted, the Huddy marker stood. The Flames' powerplay failed to score on the major. From that moment on, Calgary was a beaten team. The Oilers skated to a 4–2 win, and the Bullard incident started a war of words between the Flames and Oilers.

Bullard was carried off the ice on a stretcher. Paramedics

planned to load him onto an ambulance, but Bullard opted instead to be treated by the Flames' trainers in the visitors' dressing room. "I don't even know what happened," Bullard told reporters after the loss. "I mean, I came off the bench on a line change, saw him (McSorley) swing his stick and I went down like a bag of potatoes.[57]

"The next thing I know I'm on a stretcher and they're going to put me in an ambulance," Bullard continued. "I tell them: 'Nah, just get me to the dressing room.' I didn't know what the problem was, but a couple of minutes later I sure felt sore."[58] Al MacNeil, the Flames' assistant general manager, pointed to the spear as the turning point in the series. "The referee gave them something and he gave us something," MacNeil spat. "They got the gold mine and we got the shaft."[59]

But Sather told the Edmonton papers that he felt that McSorley's actions were not premeditated. He defended the Oilers' tough guy, claiming that he was so out of sorts thanks to the Roberts hit, he didn't have control of his mental faculties. "I don't think Marty knew what he did. I saw him get hit into the boards and the next thing I knew he was on the end of the bench and he was out cold."[60]

Flames forward Perry Berezan says that, injured or not, the Flames tried to use the incident as a rallying point. "The stick kind of went through Mike. And we all talked about how we had to go out and get the Oilers for Mike, even though we knew he wasn't hurt."

McSorley and Bullard were not the only casualties in the game. Berezan was KO'd by a crushing check from Mark Messier. Late in the game, Tim Hunter tried to inflict his own style of cowboy justice on the Oilers when he ran into netminder Grant Fuhr. Hunter got a major for his effort.

With the Oilers up in the series three games to none, Game 4 was one of the most anticlimactic match-ups in the history of the rivalry. The Flames' hearts were clearly not in it early, as the Oilers took a commanding 4–0 lead and eventually held on for a 6–4 triumph.

After the series was over, the NHL reviewed the McSorley spear and deemed that it was severe enough to earn the Oiler a three-game suspension. For the Flames, it was too little, too late. "It is my assessment that McSorley deliberately speared his opponent (Bullard) for no apparent reason and used enough force to cause an injury," stated NHL vice-president Brian O'Neill in a media release. "There is no justification for any player to use his stick in this manner."

Berezan sums up the Flames frustration at the time. "In 1987 and '88, we had such a great team; it was just that Edmonton had a better team."

The Oilers would use the momentum gained in the Battle of Alberta to win their fourth Cup in five years in one of the oddest Stanley Cup finals ever. Poised to sweep the Bruins at the old Boston Garden, Game 4 was cancelled with the score tied in the second period when the power went out in the old Original Six building. NHL president John Ziegler ordered Game 4 to be replayed in Edmonton, where the Oilers got the chance to celebrate their victory in front of their home fans.

But while the Oilers carried the Cup after beating the Bruins, Simpson says that the sweep of the Flames was the key to the team's fourth championship in five seasons. "The way that we beat the Flames, to sweep the series and to win the first two games on the road, we knew that we were on our way to the Cup. In '88, before the series started, we knew that if we were able to beat them, we would win the Cup...I think what was a big part of our team that season is how we could go on the road and have success. Being able to win on the road is one of the traits of a great team. And both of those wins in Calgary were very tough wins. The second game was won in overtime and I think the first game was won in the last few minutes. And that held true in the finals; we went five wins and no losses in the Boston Garden in the finals in 1988 and 1990. And the funny thing is that we went 0–6 during that time span in the regular season."

Gretzky and McSorley were the two pivotal players in the '88 Battle of Alberta. At the time, little did either know it would be their last Battle of Alberta. On August 9, 1988, in a move spurred by Oilers' owner Peter Pocklington's ongoing financial difficulties, both McSorley and Gretzky were sent to the Los Angeles Kings in the most significant trade in the history of professional sports.

While Edmonton reeled over the loss of their favourite adopted son, Calgary general manager Cliff Fletcher continued to tinker with his lineup. The Flames emerged as one of the NHL's dominant teams in 1988–89, and would not be denied. The Oilers, ironically, would be eliminated by Gretzky and the Kings in the 1989 playoffs. But no team would be a match for the Flames, who would become the only road team to ever win the Cup on hallowed Montreal Forum ice, with MacInnis winning the Conn Smythe Trophy for the playoff MVP.

That Cup win was oh-so-satisfying for Tim Hunter, who

had become all too used to hearing how the Flames, unlike the Oilers, couldn't win the big game. The Cup changed all of that. "They were better than us, but we became as good as they were," he says. "We didn't have the same kind of talent as they did, but we came together as a team. Really, it was the two greatest teams in the NHL at the time playing in the same division."

But the Oilers rebounded in 1990. Despite being heavy underdogs and forced to use the unproven Bill Ranford in goal, the Oilers won their fifth Cup, proving that they were still a power without the Great One. Ranford would win the Conn Smythe for his stellar play.

The Cup split between the two clubs in the years immediately following Gretzky's departure kept the Battle at a boil. Those circumstances would make for yet another thrilling instalment of the greatest rivalry in hockey in 1991.

Dave Brown—Fists of Fury

There have been some awfully exciting fights throughout the history of the Flames/Oilers rivalry, featuring the likes of Dave Semenko, Paul Baxter, Kevin McClelland, Tim Hunter, Marty McSorley and Jim Peplinski. When you ask players and fans which fights they remember best, though, one former Oiler tough guy's name comes to the top of the list—Dave Brown. He wasn't with the Oilers nearly as long as Semenko, McClelland or McSorley—he won just one Cup with the team. But he sure made a reputation for himself in the short time he was in Edmonton after being dealt to the Oilers from the Philadelphia Flyers. Brown spent two and a half seasons with the Oilers from 1989–91, a time when the 6′5″ native of Saskatoon was known to be the coldest-blooded fighter in all of hockey, with fists that mashed heads with the power of piledrivers.

"Dave Brown." Those two words placed together evoke the same kind of fear as "Ogie Oglethorpe" when hockey's greatest fictitious tough guy skates out for his cameo in the classic film *Slap Shot*. Brown's two classic fights—with

Flames tough guys Stu Grimson in 1990 and Jim Kyte in 1991—are continually remembered as two of the scariest moments in the history of the Battle of Alberta.

The Flames knew they needed a heavyweight who could stand up to Brown. Calgary summoned Stu Grimson from the Salt Lake Golden Eagles of the International Hockey League. In 62 games in Salt Lake that season, "The Grim Reaper" amassed a whopping 319 penalty minutes, and boasted an undefeated fight record in his IHL career.

"With Brownie, we had established our nuclear power," recalls Craig MacTavish, the Oilers' current head coach who was part of the '89–'90 Cup champion team. "We all knew why Grimson was called up to the Flames, to be their nuclear power."

Grimson was inserted into the lineup for the Flames' January 7, 1990 trip to Northlands Coliseum. He and Brown got into two fights that night. Brown, who had just had stitches taken out of a cut over his eye, was vulnerable. Grimson caught him with a punch that reopened the cut. That one blow had Calgary coach Terry Crisp, the Calgary media and Grimson himself claiming a victory. The Oilers players felt Brown should still have been awarded a TKO win despite the blood. Grimson's exploits were made all that much greater by the fact that the Oilers put out arguably their worst effort of the season. The Flames won the showdown in Edmonton by a 3–1 count.

The Oilers knew they would have a chance to redeem themselves with a rematch at the Saddledome two nights later. The boasts from the Calgary press and the Flames that Grimson had not only stood his ground but had actually beaten Brown only served to stir the Oilers and their top fighter. "I think the worst thing that happened was what the Calgary press did to Grimson," says MacTavish. "They said that Grimson had fared well in his battle with Dave Brown, that he had stood up to Dave Brown. And that really motivated Brownie for the next game."

"Really, to be fair, the first fight was a draw," recalls then-Oilers defenceman Craig Muni. "But when Stu reacted the way he did, it really riled up the team, so it was really quite a battle the next day."

Brown warned reporters that Grimson had best be prepared for round two. The day before the rematch in Calgary, Brown jokingly warned reporters not to take their eyes off the ice when the Flames and Oilers met again. "Don't be leaving for coffee, huh?"[61]

Four minutes after the puck dropped at the Saddledome, Brown squared off against Grimson and delivered a series of violent blows to the Grim Reaper's face. He administered a beating that still has his teammates in awe to this day. One shot would break Grimson's jaw. The beating helped motivate the Oilers to a 3–2 overtime win, showing that revenge is indeed a dish best served cold. Martin Gélinas netted the winner.

"In the third go-round, Brown looked like a cross between Don Rickles and Mike Tyson," wrote *Calgary Herald* columnist Allan Maki.[62] "He pulverized then roasted Grimson."

Lyle "Sparky" Kulchisky, who has worked in the Oilers dressing room from the team's glory days to today, says that Grimson deserves a nod for the way he handled himself after being badly beaten. "You have to give Grimson credit. After the fight, he skated to the penalty box and served the full five minutes. He had a broken jaw but he stayed in the box. After he served his time, he skated off the ice, took off his skates and equipment and then went to the hospital."

To this day, Brown downplays the beating he gave to Grimson on that night. "Really, it was two guys doing what they were supposed to do. I didn't think it was a big deal at all, but the media made a big deal out of it. It was made to be a lot more than it was."

That view wasn't shared by Bill Ranford, who was the Oilers starting goalie that night and the man who would go on to win the Conn Smythe trophy as the playoff MVP when the Oilers captured the Cup later that year. "Brown had it in his mind to destroy him," Ranford said to reporters after the game.[63]

Brown's second main event came a year later, as the defending Cup champion Oilers faced the Flames in the first round of the 1991 playoffs. The Flames, who had finished ahead of the Oilers in the standings, were trailing 2–1 in the series, which was surprisingly fight-free until Game 4.

Flames defenceman Jim Kyte was a rough customer, but he wasn't an esteemed fighter like Tim Hunter or Grimson. He never eclipsed 200 penalty minutes in his entire NHL career, which also included stops with the Winnipeg Jets, Pittsburgh Penguins, Ottawa Senators and San Jose Sharks. But the playoffs have a funny way of bringing out the bravery in players, and Kyte found himself grappling with Brown in what was the first bout of the 1991 Battle of Alberta.

Brown had done enough to knock Kyte to the ice, but according to eyewitness MacTavish, Kyte landed a punch on the way down, which incensed Brown enough to keep throwing punches even after the Flames defenceman was laid out on the ice. The beating was bad enough that MacTavish skated over to plead with his teammate show Kyte some mercy.

"I was on the ice when he had the fight with Jim Kyte," recalls MacTavish. "Brownie knocked him down, but he kept feeding him punches; he was pounding him while he was still on the ice. I was yelling for Brownie to stop. The funny thing is that, two years later, Kyte tried to sucker me at centre ice, and I felt kind of sorry that I helped him!"

Kyte was seen by reporters the next day with his shoulder in a harness and his face badly swollen. Kyte admitted to reporters that he was ill-prepared to battle Brown, who as a left-hander posed an unorthodox challenge to most NHL scrappers. "You know you have to hold on to it (the left hand). But I couldn't do it."[64]

Today, Brown has no ill will towards either Grimson or Kyte. All he will say is that both the Grim Reaper and Kyte were battlers, symbols of the kind of steely resistance the Flames regularly gave the Oilers. Even Brown admits that the Flames would have a few championships more in the team record book if the timing had been better—had Calgary not enjoyed its glory years at the same time as Edmonton.

"I think it (the severity of the fights) was the fact that both teams were so very good," says Brown. "We were very close in all senses. They had some of the best players in the game. Really, if it wasn't for Edmonton, Calgary might have had a Cup more or two."

Grimson recovered from his injuries to play 729 career NHL games and amass 2,113 career penalty minutes.

Ironically, Grimson's career would come to an end during the 2000–01 season. A severe concussion inflicted by the fists of then-Oilers enforcer Georges Laraque put the KO on Grimson, who was the policeman for the Nashville Predators at the time.

1991—Esa's in Seventh Heaven

For fans on the northern side of the Battle of Alberta, maybe the greatest instalment of the classic rivalry came in a year that the Oilers didn't win the Stanley Cup.

The year was 1991—and the Oilers were the defending Cup champs. The team had to face the difficult task of taking on the Flames in the first round of the playoffs, with home ice advantage in Calgary's favour. The Oilers had finished the season third in the Smythe Division with a .500 record, 20 points behind the Flames. The Oilers were very much a team in a state of flux. Their scoring power had waned, and the '90–'91 season marked the first time in their NHL lives that the Oilers did not score 300 goals in a season.

But the form sheet went out the window once the series began. During the first four games of the Battle of Alberta, the Flames gave no indication that they had finished with 20 more points and had scored 72 more goals than the Oilers through the regular season. After the Oilers took a three-games-to-one lead in the series, outscoring the Flames by a 13–9 count in the first four games, the Oilers looked good to wrap up the series on Saddledome ice. The series had, so far, been an unusual one as compared to other Calgary/Edmonton battles. Until left-handed Oilers enforcer Dave Brown laid a beating on Jim Kyte in Edmonton's 5–2 Game 4 win, the Battle of Alberta had gone without a fight.

Up to that point, the most talked about skirmish during the series happened off the ice, when Flames goaltending coach Glenn Hall, the former Edmonton Flyers and National Hockey League legend, confronted *Calgary Herald* writer Gyle Konotopetz in a corridor outside the Flames' dressing room. A screaming match ensued. After the Kyte/Brown fight, the series gained in intensity, and the Flames turned what looked to be an Oilers rout into a classic.

"In terms of memories, I would say that Gretkzy's goal in '88 was the most special moment in the Battle of Alberta," recalls Craig Simpson, who had netted 30 goals that season for the Oilers. "But the '91 series was the most challenging, nastiest series I've ever been a part of. We were the defending Cup champs, and that was the last year that they had the core nucleus of guys who had been part of the glory days of the Battle."

It was in Game 5 that the Flames, led by diminutive forward Theoren Fleury, got back into the series. A game-winning goal from defenceman Rick Nattress pushed the Flames to a 5–3 win in front of their home fans, and in truth the game shouldn't have been that close. While the Oilers still held a large advantage in the series, there was no escaping the feeling that somehow the Flames had turned the tide and snatched the momentum away from their most-hated rivals.

The series was a prime example of just why Oilers/ Flames playoff series were so good. "One thing about our playoff series is that because we played in the old Smythe Division together, we'd always face each other early, in the first or second round," recalls former Oiler three-time Cup winner Craig MacTavish. "Both teams were still fresh, not like the Cup final, when both teams are already exhausted when they get there."

Tough guy Ron Stern, who played with the Flames until 1997, was acquired at the 1991 trade deadline from Vancouver to add some strength to the Calgary lineup for the post-season push. "Risebrough took me aside before the series started," says Stern, referring to new Flames coach Doug Risebrough. "He said, 'I don't know how much you know about the Battle of Alberta. But we are going to win, and it's going to go seven games. And you are going to feel it.' It was by far the most intense hockey I had ever played. The referees let anything and everything go. You played hard because you knew you weren't going to get any favours from the ref. You had to take your lumps and keep going. I can't remember anything in the past that was like playing against that lineup. Yes, I had played against them when I was in Vancouver, but that was a totally different situation than playing them as a Calgary Flame. As a Flame, when you played Edmonton, you anticipated a win. In Vancouver, all we worried about was damage control."

There was no denying that there was a feeling of tension throughout Northlands Coliseum as Edmonton attempted to close out the series in six games on home ice. Game 6 was not the end-to-end game that the Flames and Oilers usually came up with. Instead, it was a cautious affair with the score knotted 1-1 through regulation. Then Fleury struck in overtime. He intercepted a poor Mark Messier pass and found himself on a clear breakaway. Fleury found a spot between Grant Fuhr's legs and slid the puck past the goal line, tying the series and reestablishing Calgary as the favourite to advance. Fleury had made his coach a prophet; the series would indeed go seven games.

Fleury then engaged in the most infamous victory dance in the history of the Coliseum. He skated, arms waving, across the ice, rubbing salt into the wounds of the Edmonton fans who sat in stunned silence. Fleury dropped to his knees, slid, and finally crashed to the boards, where he was mobbed by his Flames teammates. "That skate was almost as long as the one I had on the breakaway," laughed Fleury after the game.[65]

But while Fleury's celebration displayed the jubilation felt by the Flames and their fans, to the Oilers it was a slap in the face. To the Oilers, Fleury's victory lap was nothing more than hot-dogging, and inappropriate as the Flames hadn't won the series yet. "It (Fleury's dance) was a shot in the arm," remembers Oilers defenceman Craig Muni.

If the Fleury dance was supposed to act as a motivator for the Oilers, they surely didn't show it early on in Game 7. The 20,176 fans packed into the Saddledome erupted into premature celebrations when the Flames took an early 3–0 lead. In the process of getting that lead, Fleury did yet another victory dance on the ice, pumping his fists in front of the Oilers bench. It was this second demonstration that got the Oilers' attention.

"I can recall it was a packed house," says Brown. "There was a lot of excitement; it was a very intense game. And then Fleury scored in the first period and he started to fly around the ice pumping his arms." The comeback was on. The Oilers, thanks to two goals from Finnish superpest Esa Tikkanen, tied the game 3–3 before the end of the second period. Then, seldom-used Russian Anatoli Semenov scored to give the Oilers the third-period lead.

The Flames, regaining their composure after the Semenov goal, dominated the play for the remainder of the third. With less than five minutes to go in the game, the Flames could not bang the puck past Fuhr. But it just would not have been a proper Battle of Alberta had the series concluded without yet another plot twist. With just a little over two minutes left in regulation, Al MacInnis, the Flame who boasted the hardest shot in the league, let one of his feared slappers fly at the goal. It missed the target, but the puck bounced to Stern, who managed to bang the puck past Fuhr and send the sellout crowd into raptures.

Stern's goal may have only served to set up an even larger heartbreak for Flames fans. At 6:56 of overtime, the majority of the Saddledome crowd, some of whom had paid up to $1,000 for a scalped ticket, were crestfallen when Tikkanen completed the hat trick.

"I think the greatest moment in the rivalry, for me, was being down to Calgary 3–0 and coming back to win in overtime," reminisces Brown. While Brown says that winning in the Saddledome doesn't quite compare to being part of the '90 Oilers team that won the fifth Cup in franchise history—the only one sans Wayne Gretzky—he can still vividly recall the night of April 16, 1991.

"That was an awfully good lesson on how things can change in a series," recalls Simpson. "Any time you are down 3–0 in Game 7 on the road after only 12 minutes, winning a game is definitely not an easy task. But we found a way."

But the Flames series would have an overall negative effect on the Oilers. The Flames had pushed them so hard, they had little left for the rest of the playoffs. The Oilers ousted Gretzky and his Los Angeles Kings in six games to take the Smythe Division crown, but four of the six went into overtime.

Muni recalls that when the Oilers faced the Minnesota North Stars for the Campbell Conference crown and the right to play the Pittsburgh Penguins in the Cup final, the team's energy resources were depleted. "Our experience in the West was that we always had to go through Calgary to get to the finals. But I remember when we lost to Minnesota in the Conference Finals, we had a real long series against Calgary, where we battled very hard. In fact, we had two long battles before Minnesota. We let our guard down against Minnesota, we thought things would get easier. They got on us before we could get our breath. Before we knew it, the series was over."

The North Stars, led by goaltender Jon Casey, whipped the Oilers in five games. The Stars shredded the Oilers defence for 20 goals. Even though Minnesota had finished the 1991 regular season 12 games under .500 and had squeaked into the playoffs thanks to the fact that the sad-sack Toronto Maple Leafs finished 23 games under .500, they had more than enough left in the tank to overcome an exhausted Oilers bunch.

The Battle of Alberta Transformed

The famous 1991 Battle of Alberta series would mark the end of an era. Esa Tikkanen's Game 7 overtime winner would not only shock the Flames fans who jammed the Saddledome, it would also be the last shot fired between the two teams in a game outside of the NHL regular season or exhibition schedule.

While the Oilers were defending Cup champs in 1990, the club was already wrestling with the economic realities of the modern NHL. The team had dealt Wayne Gretzky to Los Angeles in 1988, and soon the entire core of the dynasty would be playing hockey in more lucrative big-city markets. Mark Messier would become a fan favourite on Broadway and deliver the Rangers a Stanley Cup in 1994 on a team that also included ex-Oilers Kevin Lowe, Glenn Anderson, Adam Graves, Craig MacTavish, Esa Tikkanen and Jeff Beukeboom. Jari Kurri would go from Los Angeles to New York to Anaheim to Denver.

The Oilers didn't win the Cup in 1991, but made the playoffs again in 1992. Devastated by dwindling crowds and a slumping Canadian dollar, team president and general manager Glen Sather was forced to face the reality that the team would need to rebuild—and that all of the high-priced veteran talent would have to be allowed to leave as free agents or traded away for cheaper prospects and draft picks.

From 1993–96, Edmonton was a place devoid of playoff hockey. As the era of superstars gave way to a new generation of unproven talent, the question in Edmonton changed from how far the Oilers would go in the playoffs to whether the city would be able to keep NHL hockey. The signs from other small Canadian markets were not encouraging. In 1995, Quebec City lost its Nordiques to Denver. A year later, the Winnipeg Jets would pull up their stakes and head south the Phoenix. As player salaries escalated and the Canadian dollar continued to sag, the cost of doing hockey business in any Canadian city other than Toronto became more and more prohibitive every year, and the lure of a large, untapped American market grew stronger.

The Flames would return to the playoffs every season until 1996, but would continue to confound their fans by not making it out of the first round. From 1997–2003, the team never got to the post-season. In fact, since 1989, when the franchise became the only visiting team to ever win the Stanley Cup in the hallowed Montreal Forum, the Flames did not win a single playoff round until 2004. Like the Oilers, the Flames soon lost grip of their core players. Al MacInnis, the rearguard with the hardest slapper in hockey, would spend most of the '90s with the St. Louis Blues. Joe Nieuwendyk was traded away to the Dallas Stars; Joe Mullen won two more Cups with Mario Lemieux and the Pittsburgh Penguins and Mike Vernon would win the Conn

Smythe Trophy as playoff MVP in 1997 as a member of the cash-splashing Detroit Red Wings. Then came the cruelest blow of all; Theoren Fleury, the man who had been the poster boy for Flames hockey for the better part of a decade, was soon to grow into a contract that would be too fat for the Flames to maintain. So, at the 1999 trade deadline, he was dispatched to the Colorado Avalanche.

As the Flames faded from the playoff landscape in 1997, the Oilers returned with a team based on youth, speed and a couple of blue-chip (and affordable) twentysomethings in forwards Ryan Smyth and Doug Weight. Smyth was a native Albertan, a kid who bled Oilers blue from childhood—the kind of player who could score 30 times a year by taking punishment in front of the opposition net and collecting those garbage goals. Weight was the flashy American playmaker, an articulate leader and student of the game claimed in a trade that sent Tikkanen to the Rangers. Weight soon become a natural choice to be the next Oilers' captain. The pair would spearhead a renaissance in Edmonton and a return to playoff hockey.

The spring of 1997 not only saw a major changing of the guard in Alberta hockey—the Oilers returning to playoff form, the Flames out of the post-season for only the second time since arriving in Calgary from Atlanta—but also a change in priorities. Like the Oilers, the Flames were falling on hard financial times. While rumours of an imminent move to the United States did not circulate in the Calgary papers as they did in Edmonton, the Flames were really in no better shape than the Oilers to cope with a new NHL, in which the large-market American clubs could try and buy themselves the Stanley Cup.

Rather than remaining fierce combatants from North and South—oil town vs. government town, Rocky Mountains vs. prairies—fans in Calgary and Edmonton no longer saw the other as Public Enemy Number One. Yes, the Flaming C and the Oil Drop were still symbols of opposing tribes—but a bigger battle was on the horizon: the struggle to keep the Battle of Alberta going. After all, a team is defined by its rivals—what would the Red Sox be without the Yankees? Who would Packers fans learn to hate if the Bears weren't around? Or could you imagine the city of Milan without the annual soccer battles between the striped shirts of A.C. and Inter?

If either the Flames or the Oilers were to follow the same path south taken by the Nordiques and Jets, the Battle would be lost. After watching thousands of Winnipeggers weep as they waved goodbye to their Jets after the team was eliminated at home in the '96 playoffs by Detroit, Edmontonians and Calgarians knew that they could be the next ones to lose their teams. So, while remaining enemies on the ice, Flames and Oilers fans realized they shared an even deeper pain—the worry of losing a team.

When the Oilers opened the 1997 playoffs, the city was drunk with hatred for a new enemy: the Dallas Stars. The Stars were the symbol of the new NHL. In 1993, businessman Norm Green (ironically, an Albertan, and a key member of the group that brought the Flames to Calgary in 1980) uprooted the Minnesota North Stars from the Twin Cities—a place where hockey is as revered as it is in Canada—and moved the franchise to Dallas, a city that gushed with oil money.

Dallas and Edmonton would play the most fondly

remembered playoff series outside of a Stanley Cup win in Oilers history. The Oilers won the series in Dallas's Reunion Arena in overtime of Game 7. Soon after Oilers netminder Curtis Joseph robbed former Flame Joe Nieuwendyk by sprawling across the crease—you can still hear *Hockey Night in Canada*'s Bob Cole yelling "Oh, my goodness!" into the mic—Todd Marchant took a Doug Weight pass and used a speed burst to get around Stars defender Grant Ledyard. Marchant then roofed the game-winner past former Oiler Andy Moog in the Dallas net.

The Oilers won three of their four games against Dallas in overtime. After trailing 3–0 in the final five minutes of Game 3, Doug Weight, Andrei Kovalenko and Mike Grier all scored in the span of 1:56 to send the game into overtime, where Kelly Buchberger iced it for the Oilers. "That's definitely the most exciting game I've ever been a part of," said Grier. "When Dougie scored, we knew on the bench that we could come back and win that one. When Andrei came back and made it a one-goal game, we knew we were going to come back."

Ryan Smyth scored the double OT winner through Moog's legs to win Game 5.

The Stars did not take defeat lightly. In 1998, a retooled Stars team, with Ed Belfour replacing Moog in net, beat the Oilers in five games after Edmonton had upset the Colorado Avalanche in the first round. Between 1997 and 2003, the Oilers and Stars battled each other in six separate playoff series. Dallas won every round but that first one in '97— talk about revenge.

"The only rivalry I have ever played in that was close to this was the old Montreal/Quebec games," said Stars forward Kirk Muller in 2003—who won a Cup with the Canadiens back in '93. "No matter what province they are from, whether they are from east or west, every hockey fan looks forward to the Edmonton/Dallas series, because it is great playoff hockey."

With each passing defeat, Edmonton's contempt for the Stars grew. Because Calgary missed the playoffs year after year, the Flames had been supplanted by the Stars as Oilers' fans Public Enemy Number One.

One season after the Oilers' remarkable upset of the Stars, Oilers fans got an even bigger boost—the saving of their team from American investors. Owner Peter Pocklington's assets were seized by the Alberta Treasury Branch, and in early 1998, the only significant offer that had come to the ATB for the Oilers had been tabled by Les Alexander, a Houston-based sports magnate whose empire also included the Rockets of the National Basketball Association. While Alexander publicly pledged that he would try and keep the Oilers in Edmonton, the city's hockey fans dreaded that they would soon be joining Winnipeg and Quebec City as small-market Canadian cities that had lost their hockey teams to America.

A large group of businesspeople led by Gasland head Cal Nichols tendered a counteroffer for the team at the ninth hour. On March 13, 1998, the Edmonton Investors Group, which also included high-profile business leaders like Bruce Saville, Jim Hole and famed comic-book creator (and the man behind the famous *Spawn* franchise) Todd McFarlane, placed the necessary $5 million deposit with the ATB. By the ATB's own bylaws, if an Alberta-based investor came forward with a realistic offer, the ATB would have to go with that over any foreign deals. The loophole guaranteed that, as long as the EIG came up with the necessary dough, the Oilers would be saved.

The EIG continue to own the Oilers to this day, and they have brought some stability to the franchise, even though the group stood tough in its support of a NHL-mandated salary cap which led to an ugly lockout of players that began in the fall of 2004 and cancelled the entirety of the 2004–05 season. To keep hockey alive in Edmonton, Nichols and his group have had to keep a close watch on the pursestrings—the team simply doesn't have the budget to compete with the likes of the New York Rangers, Colorado Avalanche or Detroit Red Wings. Instead, the Oilers' made the playoffs six times from 1997–2003 because of shrewd management with a knack for recognizing young talent. The team had to trade away or let slip into free agency stars such as Weight, Bill Guerin and Curtis Joseph, but Oilers fans have been supportive, recognizing the limitations of the Canadian dollar and the financial constraints that come with being a Canadian city of fewer than one million people.

While the Oilers underwent a Renaissance, the Flames began their rebuilding plans in the most ironic of ways. The Flames opened the 1997–98 season with a new, young roster. Seven of the Flames on the roster—Ed Ward, tough guy Chris Dingman, veteran defenceman Zarley Zalapski, hard-nosed Todd Simpson, two-way forward Cale Hulse, upstart defender Derek Morris and future superstar Jarome Iginla—all listed Edmonton as their place of birth. "Yeah, it's something we joke about all the time," laughed Iginla during the 1997 preseason. "We're all aware about how many guys on this team come from Edmonton. We know whenever we play Edmonton that it's a big game. When we come to Edmonton, we like to play hard because we have all those friends and family to impress...It's great that I can still play so close to my home. My family and friends can come and see me play. But I know that it's kind of funny for them, the situation that they're in. They all still have a hard time cheering for the Flames because they live in Edmonton."

Zalapski, who grew up near Edmonton International Airport in the southern suburb of Leduc and played his junior hockey in the Edmonton east satellite of Fort Saskatchewan, said that even his close friends told him that they would not change allegiances from the Oil to the Flames. "It's just the way you look at it," said Zalapski, who played in Calgary a decade earlier as part of the Canadian national team that took part in the 1988 Winter Olympics. "I see my friends watching me play and they see me playing for the 'other' side. If people want to call us Alberta's real home team, that's fine. Most of my friends are still Oilers fans. I'm not going to change that. They joke around with me about being a Flame, but it's something I don't take too seriously. I certainly understand that it's part of the rivalry, but I don't make a big deal about it. The Flames are my team. That's that."

In 2004, Morris, then a member of the Phoenix Coyotes, reminisced about how he grew up dreaming about being the next Paul Coffey. "Growing up in a small town near Edmonton, everyone followed the Oilers. If you were a forward, you dreamed about being Wayne Gretzky. If you were a defenceman, you dreamed about being Paul Coffey."

Not only did the Flames sign Edmonton-born players,

they also acquired ex-Oilers. Grant Fuhr and Steve Smith, two men who had played such large roles in Edmonton during the glory days of the Battle, both finished their careers in Calgary. Fuhr's final game came in the last-regular season match-up of the '99–'00 season, at the Saddledome against the Oilers. He was pencilled in as the backup, but after the Oilers took an early lead, both Calgary and Edmonton fans called "Fuhr, Fuhr, Fuhr!" in the hopes that Flames coach Brian Sutter would put him between the pipes for one last Battle of Alberta curtain call. Fuhr played the rest of the game and received an ovation after every save.

"It's different now," says Fuhr. "Both Smitty and myself went to Calgary. The way the teams were with each other 10 years ago, that would have never happened."

But the Flames' rebirth did little to soothe Flames fans, who had grown cynical throughout the late '90s. By 2000, the team's season ticket base had fallen below 10,000—and soon Flames fans were faced with the same reality as Oiler fans had endured just a few years before, that their team could leave town. The city responded with the "Flames Forever" campaign, which saw season ticket numbers rise from 10,000 to over 14,000.

Meanwhile, the Oilers began an Alberta retooling of their own in 2000. After Sather left Edmonton to pursue life as the head of the New York Rangers, the Edmonton Investors Group decided to hire an Alberta-born-and-bred replacement. Patrick LaForge, who grew up in Lac La Biche, northeast of Edmonton, was brought in as the new president, while Kevin Lowe—who coached the team the previous season and had won five Stanley Cups as an Oiler—was named the new general manager. Lowe had spent much of the '90s with the Rangers, including the team's '94 Cup win.

"I've been with the Oilers as either a player or coach for the last four years since I returned from New York City," he said. "They have all been very exciting years, four play-off appearances—and twice we upset number-one ranked teams. The team has improved throughout. We've laid the groundwork to win."

LaForge pointed out that Edmonton should feel blessed to have an NHL team—to be part of an exclusive club that allowed it to get mentioned alongside the major metropolises of North America. LaForge undertook a new plan that would increase the Oilers' presence in the community, to do more charitable work and to increase the customer-service aspects of the franchise. Between the two, the Oilers were able to create a revolution of sorts, refiring Edmontonians' passion for the Oilers to the levels of the '80s. In 2004, *ESPN the Magazine* rated the Oilers as one of the top 10 franchises in all of North American pro sport, not a bad feat for a team that hadn't been past the first round of the playoffs since 1998.

"In North America, I've counted about 53 cities that have a population of 900,000 or more," LaForge said. "Only 30 have the privilege of being NHL cities. Think about what the NHL means to a city; could you name many of the other 23? We are in an exclusive club with places like Los Angeles, New York, Dallas, Toronto and Chicago."

When Lowe was appointed GM, Ryan Smyth and Jason Smith were the team's two senior Alberta-born corner-stones. Almost immediately, Lowe began upping the Alberta content of the team. He would add a series of Alberta-born players to the Oilers' stable, following the Flames' game plan. Camrose natives Josh Green and Scott Ferguson worked their way onto the team, as did Calgarian Domenic Pittis. Calgary's Smith would become the Oilers captain. Edmontonians Fernando Pisani and Jason Chimera were added. Edmontonian Mike Comrie, hailed as one of the top prospects of the game, was signed in a December 2000 deal that prevented the centre—who could have re-entered the draft in 2000—from slipping through Lowe's fingers. Comrie immediately became the Oilers' poster boy, the wunderkind who was running away with the Western Hockey League scoring race at the time he decided to come to the NHL.

Comrie was the centrepiece of the new "Alberta" Oilers, so the city and franchise were badly stung in 2003 when Comrie and agent Rich Winter asked for a trade, citing personal reasons that were not made public. Comrie was eventually dealt to the Philadelphia Flyers for defence prospect Jeff Woywitka, who had played his junior hockey just down Highway 2 in Red Deer. Comrie remained in Philly only for a few weeks, from where he was eventually dealt to Wayne Gretzky's Phoenix Coyotes.

But even though the hockey relations between the two cities were warming, there were still some flashpoints that showed that there was still some real bad blood between the franchises.

In 2002, the Oilers needed a win in their final home game of the season in order to stay alive for the eighth and final playoff spot in the west. The Flames, long eliminated from the playoff chase, would provide the opposition. The Flames would go on to a famous win. But that was not the end of the Oilers' humiliation. After the game, as part of the fan-appreciation proceedings, the Oilers players would have to stay on the ice to give their game-worn jerseys to fans who had won an in-house contest. The Oilers were in tears as fans came onto the ice to claim their jerseys. Even though the Flames were not a playoff club, they had come into Edmonton and not only quashed the Oilers' post-season hopes, but ruined the team's fan-salute night, as well.

In 2003, the focus was on the comic. During the third period of a late-season drubbing at the Saddledome, Flames' mascot Harvey the Hound came to the Oilers bench to heckle coach Craig MacTavish. The coach turned and snatched the fake tongue on the mascot costume, ripped it off and tossed it to the crowd. The Oilers, buoyed by the incident, stormed back, and it took late heroics from Flames goalie Roman Turek to preserve a one-goal win. MacTavish became an international celebrity for the incident, and was even invited to appear on Jay Leno's famous late show in Los Angeles. MacTavish refused the invite.

Those incidents could not stop the swell of respect between the two cities' fans, which reached an all-time high in 2004. With a week left in the season, the Flames had clinched their first playoff spot since 1996 with a regular season home win over the Phoenix Coyotes. Meanwhile, the Oilers found themselves in a dogfight with the St. Louis Blues and Nashville Predators for the final two playoff spots available in the Western Conference. One of the three teams would miss while the other two would claw their way into the post-season.

The Oilers final game of the season was in Vancouver, and they needed a win in order for their hopes to stay alive. But it was not to be—the Canucks snuffed out the Oilers playoff hopes. The win cemented Vancouver's place—along with Dallas—as one of the most-hated teams in Edmonton. Canucks star Todd Bertuzzi was earlier suspended indefinitely by the NHL for an attack on Colorado Avalanche forward Steve Moore, which didn't help the Canucks' reputation in Edmonton. Nor did the presence of Matt Cooke and Jarkko Ruutu, two of the finest agitators in the NHL.

As fate would have it, the playoff seeding forced the Canucks to play the Flames in the first round. Throughout the pubs in Edmonton, the fans were glued to the series and, save for the B.C. transplants, were cheering for the Flames. At the Elephant & Castle Pub on Edmonton's trendy Whyte Avenue strip, a capacity crowd roared when Flame (and former Oiler Stanley Cup winner) Martin Gélinas deposited the series winner in overtime of Game 7. The Flames had actually become the lesser of two evils when compared to Vancouver.

It was more than ironic that Edmonton turned so strongly against the Canucks. While the Canucks were the team that officially eliminated the Oilers, it was the Flames who were more influential in Edmonton's post-season miss. In their six-game season series, Edmonton won just once against the Flames. That season series domination helped the Flames build a large cushion over the Oilers in the standings.

After the Flames upset the Detroit Red Wings—the team with the largest payroll in the NHL and who had finished in first overall in the regular season—a new sign was placed outside of Edmonton's Iron Horse Pub, simply stating—"Go Cowtown Go?" Could Edmonton fans—people who had celebrated so strongly after Glen Sather flipped the bird to the Saddledome crowd after the '91 playoff win or wept so bitterly after the Steve Smith own-goal had allowed the Flames to upset the Oil in '86—really have taken the Flames into their own hearts?

After an eight-year playoff drought, Iginla, who was nominated for the Hart Trophy as NHL MVP and whose 41 regular season goals left him in a tie for the Rocket Richard Trophy as the league's top goal-scorer, enjoyed having the Flames become Alberta's team. "It was tough going home every year and watching (the Oilers) in the playoffs," he told the *Calgary Sun.* "Especially when the Oilers, a lot of years, had stolen our spot. (But) Edmonton's a very good hockey city, too."[66]

Even as the Flames faced the Red Wings in the second round of the playoffs, Edmonton—strange as it was—remained loyal to Calgary's cause.

"There's certainly no love lost between Alberta's two principal cities, on the rink or off," read an editorial in the *Edmonton Sun.*

"Edmonton Oilers general manager Kevin Lowe demonstrated that when he appeared to be cheering for the Canucks during game 7 of the Calgary/Vancouver series.

"But in this case of this version of the Calgary Flames, we're willing to cut them some slack. Because they really are Edmonton's team. (Premier Ralph) Klein went out of his way to point a big thank-you to the people of Edmonton and area for putting such a fine group of athletes on the Saddledome ice.

"He specifically mentioned Flames star forward Jarome Iginla and club president Ken King. Iginla is a product of Edmonton and St. Albert and King was a longtime executive with this newspaper.

"But Klein could have added Mike Commodore, Andrew Ference, Martin Sonnenberg, Steve Reinprecht and Dean McAmmond as either products of Edmonton hockey or hailing from within the 780 area code.

"Not to mention the Flames' brilliant coach, Darryl Sutter, who comes from the famous hockey-playing family just down the road in Viking.

"Meanwhile, the Flames roster lists no home-grown talent...

"So...Darn, it's hard to say this...Go Flames Go—all the way to the Cup.

"But when you're parading his Lordship's tankard down Deerfoot Trail—or whatever you consider your main street—remember who got you there. And remember who will be looking for you when the Battle of Alberta resumes next fall."[67]

As the Flames prepared to play the San Jose Sharks in the Western Conference final, *Edmonton Sun* columnist Kerry Diotte gave his reasons why he was backing the Flames. "Any half-decent religious movement encourages its faithful to display charity to others. It may be hard to lend support to a Calgary-based hockey fan, but we must take pity. Edmonton's teams have triumphed over Calgary so long, it is time to let Cowtowners enjoy this brief moment of glory and be happy for them."[68]

After Calgary won the first two games of the Western Conference final, it had become Canada's Team. The

Flames were the only team from north of the 49th left in the playoffs, and it had been 11 years since the Montreal Canadiens had brought the Stanley Cup home to Canada. In Edmonton, the pro-Flames frenzy was at a higher point that any time before. To Edmontonians, it became more important to see the Cup come back to Canada than it was to see Calgary be prevented from grasping it. Gusto Burgers, one of Iginla's favourite St. Albert haunts, began serving an "Iggy Burger" in his honour, and proudly served it to a clientele dominated by Oilers fans.

"I realize that we are the only Canadian team left," said Flames forward Stéphane Yelle. "It's a great feeling that goes with it, to represent this city and Alberta. It's fun. It is the whole spirit of hockey in Canada."

"It's cool," said Flame Shean Donovan of the support from Edmonton. "When I came here, I wasn't so familiar with the Calgary/Edmonton rivalry. But I talked to my uncle in Grande Prairie, (north of Edmonton, the heart of Oilers country) and he told me there are a lot of Flames fans there. I think that shows when all is said and done, Canadians will cheer for the Canadian team. And I think that's great."

When Calgary reached the Stanley Cup Final, the first time a Canadian team had been in the final since the Vancouver Canucks lost to the New York Rangers in 1994, the Flames were branded as "Canada's Team" by the media across the country. The fact that Calgary had ended the Canadian Cup drought had taken precedence over the local rivalry. By the time the Flames faced off against the Tampa Bay Lightning in the final, Edmonton was fully behind the Flames. Flames coach Darryl Sutter said that if the tables had been turned and the Oilers had gotten to the final, he would have been 100 per cent behind them.

"Well, you got to remember Calgary is in Canada," he said during a Stanley Cup final pre-game press conference. "It's our game. They are going to get excited...If Edmonton was in the Stanley Cup final, I'd be excited—I'd be one of the Albertans that was pulling for them and excited about it. So it's part of the deal, I think. It's great for them to be able to experience this in late May, early June."

The Flames were not successful in their quest. Despite having the chance to win the Cup in Game 6 on home ice, the Flames fell to the Lightning, followed by a Game 7 loss in Tampa Bay. Game 7 would be the last NHL game played in the 2004 calendar year. In September, the 30 NHL owners initiated a lockout of players, citing rising salaries and huge losses as a reason to get a new economic system in place, one which would directly tie expenses to revenues and allow teams like Calgary and Edmonton to survive well into the 21st century and beyond. The lockout ended in the summer of 2005.

Truthfully, Edmonton and Calgary's hockey cold war had been warming since the beginning of the 21st century. In the 2002–03 season, executives from both teams got permission from the province to sell scratch-and-win lottery tickets at both the Saddledome and at Skyreach Centre (Edmonton's arena at the time) and at convenience stores and supermarkets throughout the province. The "Breakaway to Win" Lottery has helped raise needed dollars to help offset the spiraling costs of running an NHL franchise.

Oilers' president Patrick LaForge admitted that the

spirit of cooperation between the teams came out of ne-
cessity. "From a business point of view, we talk to Calgary
all the time. We have to."

Craig Simpson, the former Oilers star who would later
go on to be the team's TV-broadcast colour man and later an assistant coach with the club, says that it is great
playoff series that sow the seeds of a rivalry. During the
glory days of the Battle, playoff clashes between the two
Alberta cities were rites of spring. But because the teams
haven't met in the post-season from 1991 until the end of
the 2003–04 season, the rivalry has dulled. "It was very
rare to find two teams that were so close to each other geo-
graphically that would be the most powerful and skillful
teams in the league over a period of five or six years. Over
that five- or six-year period there were a lot of great playoff
series. And great rivalries are built in the playoffs. Because
the teams haven't met in the playoffs since '91, the rivalry
has waned somewhat."

Unless NHL economics change radically—and some sort
of balance is introduced between the large- and small-market clubs in the league, the rivalry between the Flames and
Oilers won't return to its old levels.

"It was such an exciting rivalry," recalls Cliff Fletcher,
who was the general manager of the Flames during their
glory years. "But, will there be another rivalry like it now?
That would be difficult, because of the economics. Take a
look at the Edmonton team in its prime. Today, that roster
would give you a payroll of $100 million or more."

That isn't to say the mood is warm and fuzzy between
the two cities.

True, the chasm of hatred is not as wide as it used to be. Gone are the days of Calgary firemen getting their eyes put out, the days of nasty protests and insults hurled between the cities through their respective daily newspapers. Gone are the days when police officers used to break up fights between Edmonton and Calgary players in the penalty box. Gone are the barbed wire fences and the old barns that were our churches on Saturday nights, in an era when TV was a novelty and hockey games broke the boredom of our long, harsh winters.

But the legends will live on—and well they should. From Sweeney Shriner to Norm Ullman to Mark Messier to Jarome Iginla, this province has produced its fair share of hockey legends. It has given the world the greatest hockey rivalry ever. Sorry, Leafs and Canadiens fans, but it's true.

It's still not good form to wear an Oilers jersey in Calgary, or vice versa.

And that, most hockey fans in Alberta would agree, is a good thing.

Endnotes

1 *Edmonton Bulletin*, Nov. 29, 1894, Pg. 1.
2 "Hockey match."*Calgary Herald*, Jan. 15, 1895, Pg. 4.
3 "Nary a goal." *Calgary Herald*, Mar. 8, 1895, Pg. 1.
4 "Hockey." *Edmonton Bulletin*, Jan. 2, 1896, Pg. 2.
5 *Edmonton Bulletin*, Feb. 17, 1896, Pg. 1.
6 "General News." *Edmonton Bulletin*, Jan. 20, 1896, Pg. 1.
7 "The War Rumours." *Calgary Herald*, Dec. 19, 1895, Pg. 2.
8 "Canada and the Empire." *Edmonton Bulletin*, Jan. 23, 1896, Pg. 3.
9 "Railway interests." *Calgary Herald*, Dec. 12, 1895, Pg. 2.
10 *Edmonton Bulletin*, Feb. 3, 1898, Pg. 1.
11 "Hockey game." *Calgary Herald*, Dec. 12, 1895, Pg. 4.
12 "Hockey Tournament." *Edmonton Bulletin*, Feb. 16, 1899, Pg. 4.
13 "Eye Openers." The *Eye Opener*, Jan. 28, 1905, Pg. 1.
14 "Eye Openers." The *Eye Opener*, Feb. 4, 1905, Pg. 1.
15 Zeman, Gary. "Beginning of the Alberta Amateur Hockey Association" in *Alberta On Ice*. Edmonton: GMS2, 1986, 2nd ed.
16 "Calgary hockey fans have seen last big game." *Calgary Herald*, Mar. 3, 1913, Pg. 8.
17 "Taber Cooks will probably hang up skates for season." *Calgary Herald*, Mar. 3, 1913, Pg. 8.
18 "Eskimos Are Provincial Champions—Shermans Default." *Edmonton Bulletin*, Mar. 4, 1913, Pg. 9.
19 "Edmonton Eskimos annex provincial championship." *Calgary Herald*, Mar. 4, 1913, Pg. 8.

20 "Eskimos Challenged for the Allan Cup Yesterday." Edmonton Bulletin, Mar. 6, 1913, Pg. 11.

21 "Alberta Hockey Assn. has no reason to fear result of meeting of parent body." *Edmonton Bulletin*, Dec. 22, 1920, Pg. 6.

22 "Eskimos impress fans of Calgary as greatest team playing game this season." *Edmonton Bulletin*, Dec. 26, 1920, Pg. 6.

23 Gerrie, Fraser M. "Eskimos win championship in thrilling overtime struggle." *Edmonton Journal*, Mar. 17, 1923, Pg. 28.

24 Simpson, Joe. "Simpson is still puzzled how Ottawa got the lead." *Edmonton Journal*, Mar. 30, 1923, Pg. 1.

25 "Tigers are Western Canada hockey champions." *Calgary Herald*, Mar. 8, 1924, Pg. 20.

26 "Kenny Mckenzie to sell Eskimo Hockey Team." *Edmonton Bulletin*, Mar. 23, 1925, Pg. 5.

27 "More than 2,000 jobless get relief." *Calgary Herald*, Nov. 1, 1932, Pg. 9.

28 Lewis, Bill. "Eskimos crowned champions." *Edmonton Bulletin*, Mar. 29, 1933, Pg. 10.

29 "Bengals Smother Eskimos, 8-5." *Calgary Herald*, Dec. 11, 1933, Pg. 6.

30 Lewis, Bill. "Alberta Senior Title still undecided though Bronks win." *Edmonton Bulletin*, Mar. 2, 1932, Pg. 12.

31 "Bronks' Victory Protested." *Calgary Herald*, Mar. 2, 1932, Pg. 6.

32 "Bronks' Victory Protested." *Calgary Herald*, Mar. 2, 1932, Pg. 6.

33 Lewis, Bill. "Pats and Pans." *Edmonton Bulletin*, Mar. 3, 1932, Pg. 12.

34 Mamini, Bob. "Three Straight, Which Way?" *Calgary Herald*, Mar. 26, 1946, Pg. 15.

35 Mamini, Bob. "Clever Team Effort Brings Allan Cup to Calgary." *Calgary Herald*, Apr. 29, 1946, Pg. 15.

36 "City Greets Champions." *Calgary Herald*, Apr. 29, 1946, Pg. 1.

37 Mamini, Bob. "Stampeders Make it Great Year for West." *Calgary Herald*, Apr. 29, 1946, Pg. 15.

38 Mackintosh, George. "The Sporting Periscope." *Edmonton Journal*, Mar. 22, 1948, Pg. 6.

39 Fleming, Don. "From the Sports Mill." *Edmonton Journal*, May 7, 1948, Pg. 10.

[40] "Flyers Need To Make Poile Prophet."*Edmonton Journal*, Mar. 6, 1953, Pg. 15.

[41] Fleming, Don. "Flyers Seek Two-Game Lead Tonight." *Edmonton Journal*, Mar. 26, 1953, Pg. 15.

[42] Fleming, Don "Stampeders Sabotage Flyers 4-2 To Stay In Contention." *Edmonton Journal*, Mar. 30, 1953, Pg. 20.

[43] Hunter, Gorde. "The Neutral Zone." *Calgary Herald*, Apr. 7, 1954, Pg. 34.

[44] Hunter, Gorde "The Neutral Zone." *Calgary Herald*, Apr. 15, 1954, Pg. 28.

[45] Hunter, Gorde "The Neutral Zone." *Calgary Herald*, Apr. 20, 1954, Pg. 24.

[46] "All together now, boooooo!!!" *Calgary Herald*, Apr. 6, 1962, Pg. 13.

[47] Bilych, George. "World of Sport." *Calgary Herald*, Apr. 3, 1962, Pg. 12.

[48] Bilych, George. "Poile insists Flyers 'a cinch'." *Calgary Herald*, Apr. 9, 1962, Pg. 8.

[49] Matheson, Jim. "Flames bewildered by blazing Oilers." *Edmonton Journal*, Apr. 21, 1983, Pg. F1.

[50] "Risebrough earns Sather's ire." *Edmonton Journal*, Apr. 13, 1984, Pg. H1.

[51] Matheson, Jim. "Oilers gain series stranglehold." *Edmonton Journal*, Apr. 17, 1984, Pg. F1.

[52] Simmons, Steve. "Flames can't help but believe now." *Calgary Herald*, Apr. 21, 1984, Pg. F1.

[53] Cole, Cam. "Old rivalry going to dogs." *Edmonton Journal*, Jan. 4, 1986, Pg. D1.

[54] Matheson, Jim. "Oilers search for answers." *Edmonton Journal*, Apr. 24, 1986, Pg. C1.

[55] Simmons, Steve "Believe it: We're the champs." *Calgary Herald*, May 1, 1986, Pg. A1.

[56] Duhatschek, Eric. "There is no escaping playoff fever." *Calgary Herald*, Apr. 19, 1988, Pg. C3.

[57] Blair, Jeff. "Injuries take toll on forwards." *Calgary Herald*, Apr. 24, 1988, Pg. A1.

[58] Blair, Jeff. "Shock became rage as Bullard crumpled." *Calgary Herald*, Apr. 24, 1988, Pg. F1.

[59] Maki, Allan. "Crime, it seems, does pay." *Calgary Herald*, Apr. 24, 1988, Pg. F1.

[60] Cowley, Norm. "McSorley wasn't talking." *Edmonton Journal,* Apr. 24, 1988, Pg. G1.

[61] Konotopetz, Gyle "Messier matures into a role model." *Calgary Herald,* Jan. 9, 1990, Pg. E2.

[62] Maki, Allan. "Big punchline back in Brown's delivery." *Calgary Herald,* Jan. 10, 1990, Pg. C1.

[63] Konotopetz, Gyle. "Oiler lays on licking." *Calgary Herald,* Jan. 10, 1990, Pg. C1.

[64] "Brown bags Battle bout." *Edmonton Journal,* Apr. 11, 1991, Pg. F3.

[65] "Fleury burns Oilers in OT." *Edmonton Journal,* Apr. 15, 1991, Pg. D1.

[66] Saelhof, Todd, "Battle of Alberta takes a back seat." *Calgary Sun,* Apr. 22, 2004, www.slam.ca/Slam040422/nhl_caldet9-un.html.

[67] "Er...Go Flames Go?" *Edmonton Sun,* Apr. 22, 2004, Pg. 10.

[68] Diotte, Kerry, "Six reasons to root for the Flames." *Edmonton Sun,* May 9, 2004, pg. 10.7

Works Cited

Adrahtas, Tom. *Glenn Hall: The Man They Call Mr. Goalie.* Vancouver: Greystone, 2002.

Calgaryflames.com: The Official Site of the Calgary Flames. Calgary Flames Hockey Club. 11 Dec. 2004 <http://www.calgaryflames.com>.

Condon, Eileen P., ed. *Index to the Census of Canada 1891: District of Alberta.* Regina: Regina Branch—Saskatchewan Genealogical Society Inc., 1998.

Diamond, Dan, ed. *Total Stanley Cup.* Toronto: Dan Diamond and Associates, 2004.

Edmontonoilers.com. Edmonton Oilers Hockey Club. 11 June 2004 <http://www.edmontonoilers.com>.

Edmonton Oilers Heritage Web Site. 23 Feb. 2004. Edmonton Oilers Hockey Club, Heritage Community Foundation. 22 June 2004 <http:///www.oilersheritage.com>.

Gretzky, Wayne, and Rick Reilly. *Gretzky: An Autobiography.* Toronto: HarperCollins, 1990.

Hanlon, Peter, and Sean O'Brien, eds. *2003–2004 Calgary Flames Media Guide.* Calgary: Calgary Flames Hockey Club, 2003.

Herzog, Lawrence. "The Gainer Block Marks 100 Years." *Real Estate Weekly.* 20 June 2002. 20 Nov. 2004 <http://

www.rewedmonton.ca/content_view?CONTENT_
ID=125>.

Ibsen, Bruce. "From Deacon to the Duke: The Edmonton
Eskimos Hockey Club." Diss. Edmonton & District
Historical Society, 1995.

Index to the 1901 Census of Alberta (No. 202). Edmonton:
Alberta Genealogical Society: Edmonton Branch,
1999.

Knowles, Steve, ed. *Edmonton Oilers 2003/2004 Official
Guide.* Edmonton: Edmonton Oilers Hockey Club,
2003.

Legends of Hockey. 2003. Hockey Hall of Fame. 15 Oct.
2004 <http://www.legendsofhockey.net>.

Liebmann, Frank. *The Unofficial Old Western Hockey League
Homepage.* 23 May 2004. 16 Sept. 2004 <http://www.
geocities.com/texliebmann/hockey/west/timeline.
htm>.

National Hockey League Official Guide & Record Book 2004.
Toronto: Dan Diamond and Associates, 2003.

O'Donnell, Chuck. "Seventh Heaven—ten best seventh
games in Stanley Cup competitions." *Hockey Digest.*
May 2001: n. pag.

Pengrowth Saddledome. Pengrowth Saddledome. 16 Dec.
2004 <http://www.pengrowthsaddledome.com>.

*Political Movements and Events: The Events that Shaped
a Province.* Heritage Community Foundation. 22 Oct.
2004 <http://collections.ic.gc.ca/abpolitics/events/
choosing_capital1.html>.

Pölling-Vocke, Bernt. *Hockeyarenas.com.* 15 Oct. 2003. 8
Dec. 2004 <http://www.hockeyarenas.com>.

Sandor, Steven. "The F-Files." *Oilers Zone.* 15 Nov. 1997:
17+.

Stamp, Robert M. "Alberta." *The Canadian Encyclopedia.* 4
vols. Edmonton: Hurtig, 1988.

The White House. The White House, President George W. Bush. 11 Feb. 2005 <http://www.whitehouse.gov/history/presidents/gc2224.html>.

Zeman, Gary W., ed. *Alberta on Ice*. Edmonton: GMS2, 2nd, 1986.

Index

Steven Sandor is the former editor-in-chief of Edmonton's *Vue Weekly* magazine, and the former North American editor of *Face-Off*, one of Europe's largest hockey magazines. He edited *Zone*, the official magazine of the Edmonton Oilers, from 1999 to 2004. Steve has covered the arts, business, sports (especially hockey and soccer), and politics for newspapers and magazines across Canada, the United States, the United Kingdom, Hungary, and the Czech Republic—including *Alberta Venture*, *Alberta Views*, the *Edmonton Sun*, *Prague Post*, *Budapest Sun*, *ESPN the Magazine*, *Canadian Cowboy Country*, and *World Soccer*. He is a graduate of the Ryerson Journalism Program in Toronto.

More Hockey Books From Heritage House Publishing

The Game of Our Lives
Peter Gzowski

This best-selling hockey classic tells the incredible story of the Edmonton Oilers' 1980–81 season when the team was poised on the edge of greatness. "This is a classic of hockey writing." *The Globe and Mail*
$19.95 paperback. ISBN 1-894384-59-8

Going Top Shelf: An Anthology of Canadian Hockey Poetry
Michael P.J. Kennedy, editor

From Michael Ondaatje to Stompin' Tom Connors, readers will delight in this entertaining collection of wonderful hockey poems and lyrics.
$15.95 paperback. ISBN 1-894384-99-7

Simply the Best: Insights and Strategies from Great Hockey Coaches
Mike Johnston and Ryan Walter

Simply the Best delivers rare insights on success straight from the hearts and minds of winning coaches including Scotty Bowman, Marc Crawford, Jacques Demers, Ken Hitchcock, Pat Quinn, and Mike Keenan. Recognized as the greatest coaches in the game, these "elite 12" openly discuss in their own words strategies that have made them successful.
$24.95 paperback. ISBN 1-894384-81-4

Guts and Go: Great Saskatchewan Hockey Stories
Calvin Daniels

"A great read…. This book scores with profiles of many of the most famous Saskatchewan-born NHL players, and gets a big assist with stories of lesser-known players and teams." Jason Hammond, CJRT Radio
$16.95 paperback. ISBN 1-894384-80-6

Guts and Go Overtime: More Great Saskatchewan Hockey Stories
Calvin Daniels
$16.95 paperback. ISBN 1-894974-02-6

Ask for these great books at your local bookstore,
or visit www.heritagehouse.ca